Event Management

Tips and strategies

Nigel Aksel

First Edition

Nigel Aksel
Event Management: Best Tips and Terms, 2019

1st Edition
All Rights Reserved
ISBN: 9781091752597

Table of Content

Tables

Samples

Figures

Dedication

I want to dedicate this book to my sister Yulya, who works in one of the biggest retail companies of the city as a head of HR department.

I am glad that we have the same character to develop and grow our organizations. Thanking her for supporting me in many situations as a sister, colleague and advisor.

Wish her all my best in her professional life.

For whom is this book written?

This book will be useful for new and experienced event managers, specialists and professionals.

I also included tips for organizers and business people who can utilize this book in planning, organizing, monitoring and funding their events.

Moreover, state managers, who are focusing on promotion of their cities, regions and countries can use this book for many strategies and programs.

This book is full of practical materials, but it can be used as a handbook for many tips and strategies, required in various situation of organizing the international and local events.

I recommend also this book for my students, as it contains a lot of marketing and planning examples, which can be easily applied by students in any practical work or internships.

Introduction

In every culture, we have many events and activities: birthdays, marriage days, meeting days, memorial days and many other.

In the business and public sectors, we have forums, conferences and other high-level meetings. We organize them constantly to attract people for exchange of ideas, experiences and knowledges, also starting projects or discussions of many other issues.

This book is about how to organize any event in the most effective, predictable and organized way to control its flow, content and the results. It is based on my best practices to organize international and regional events in the heart of the Central Asia.

As the first initiator of the main events a decade ago, I tried to be active, including in inviting international experts and specialists for exchange, development and interaction.

Starting with Astana Economic Forum, we could realize many interesting projects for the country. Anyone can see the results of them today, especially how Kazakhstan is different from other countries of the region. Probably you will not believe it. But it is true that many of today's changes happened only because of our first event discussions.

To activate international cooperation and organize various events on a global scale were one of my first proposals to move the nation for change. I am proud that partly I can share the experiences in this book with you now.

Even today, not only one country, but also the world needs a lot of changes in terms of thinking, economic and business development. This is one of the main points why events are still demanding.

Generally, the events help to do many effects in societies, for example:

- people can get new ideas, knowledge and experiences to understand the world and change;
- they can share one's own ideas, knowledge and experiences so that other people understand them well;
- learn new skills and competences for professional growth;
- meet new people for communication and networking;
- present projects and ideas for funding and partnerships;
- attract investors and business leaders;
- stimulate tourism by word of mouth and first experiences of the international participants.
- promote a city, region and country on the international arena;
- promote an industry or company;
- promote a product, service or new brand for export and new markets;
- involve various social groups etc.

I hope this book will uncover some of the specific advantages of the events.

Using the strategies and tips of this book you can achieve the important goals of your event. They are useful, understandable and easy to apply.

Let's explore them together!

Structure of the Book

My every book I start with structure to show briefly a reader the organization of the book. It helps to understand the book's main idea and from which section it is better to start. For example, many experienced users can check the sections, in which they were not responsible in the past.

The sections start from the what is an event in fact. And it consists from a step by step logic about how to organize an event from the beginning. However, as mentioned, you can go through the sections which are more interesting for you in order to get the details you need at a time.

The structure of the book consists of the following key sections:

1) What is Event?
2) Concept
3) Architecture
4) Program
5) HR
6) Planning
7) Marketing
8) Registration
9) Event Day
10) After Event
11) Report
12) Useful links

Any professional can use this book as a handbook in organization of different events. They can find many tips and strategies, starting from planning and writing a final report. Also, they can explore materials of the international events. They can compare them with their own materials and see which one they can apply in their work.

What is Event?

We have already discussed about the events in the previous sections. Let's briefly define the event as an occasion when people gather and meet together to talk, discuss or solve any topic of their interests.

From a business point, the event is an organized gathering of the target group to achieve the goals of the event via discussions, starting projects and writing recommendations.

As the first, we have to classify the events in order to find our niche. Let's do below.

We can classify events, by the relations to our target group:

1) Family;
2) Company;
3) Business;
4) Public.

By location:

1) Local;
2) Regional;
3) International or global.

By specialization:

1) Business;
2) Economic;
3) Investment;
4) Cultural;
5) Industrial;
6) Tourism;
7) Construction;
8) Sports;
9) IT;
10) Robotics;
11) Art etc.

By purpose:

1) Networking;
2) Presentations or speeches;
3) Discussions;
4) Preparation of recommendations/solutions;
5) Investing in projects etc.

By types:

1) Meeting
2) Gathering
3) Show (concert, performance etc.)
4) Special day (anniversary, marriage day, birthday etc.)

5) Forum;
6) Fest
7) Summit;
8) Conference;
9) Round table;
10) Seminar etc.

As you can see, events have many types, and for an organizer it is important to evaluate the best one for the selection and realization.

If you can imagine the classification, it will be easier to write a concept and focus your event on a specific goal or a target group. This will lead to the best outcome and the higher revenues.

So, let's go to the next section of the book to learn about the concept of the event.

Concept of Event

Concept of the Event is a mind map of your event. It is a vision of organizing your event.

The concept should be built on several key elements such as: topic, target audience, specialization, the main attractions etc.

For example, the topic of the Annual Investment Meeting in Dubai is about foreign direct investments. Its audience is widely diverse, but the target audience is investors and businessmen from more than 140 countries. One of the main attractions are: Showcase and Investor Hub. Generally, they built up their concept, where you can exhibit your products and services, meet investors and spend time by networking with delegates of the meeting in one of the most dynamic and developing centers of the world.

To attract target audience, any event has to have a concept. The best way to prepare - you have to understand what, where, when, who, why and how you will organize your event. This rule I learned many years ago and it works well with any area and activity. Let's see how to do it and explore them with an example below.

1. **What?**

You have to understand what will be organized by you this time or permanently. For example, birthday, marriage day or forum.

You have to state your mission, goals and objectives of your event clearly. Do not forget to ask the following questions:

- Is this a marriage or jubilee event?
- Is this a birthday, or a family event?
- Is this a forum or scientific conference?
- What did your previous speakers like most about your event? What they did not like?
- Who are your target guests?
- What interests do your target group share?
- Why do they attend events like yours?
- Should your event be investor-friendly?

2. **Where?**

Analyze where is the best place to organize your event. At home, in the restaurant or congress hall, or near a river in the nature. You have to ask yourself the following questions in order to select the best place:

- How many people attend this event?
- What are the best venues in my city to show creative approach?
- How much it cost to rent a venue?
- Do people like to walk around and see the city?
- How many activities and sessions does the program include?

3. When?

Evaluate the best time for your event. In some countries, it depends on seasonal factors, weekdays or holidays etc.

The questions to asks are:

- When are the main events held around the world?
- How many countries have reserved this day for holidays or other special days?
- Is it good time for organizing at this season?
- How is the winter or summer season and vacations can influence your event?

4. Who?

Depending on your event, you have to focus on your target group. For example, artists, government specialists, IT specialists or entrepreneurs and investors are your target group. It can be also your relatives and neighbors if you are organizing a family event.

For international and business events, you have to understand also who will be your speakers and moderators, and also honorable guests and experts, who can contribute for the development of the event.

The questions to asks are:

- Who are the most important influencers, investors or experts in the world and in the country?
- What expertise are important for resolving main issue of the country or city or the business?
- What are the best knowledge centers or organizations?
- What is the budget for inviting the top influencers?

5. Why?

You have to ask yourself, why this event is important and why you have to invite your target groups for this event.

With family events it is usually clear. But for business and public events you have think about main issues in the city, region or on global scale. This should be interesting for many people in terms of experience and sharing the expertise.

The questions to asks are:

- What are the main trends in the world?
- What are the main issues we face in economy, business, politics or in technology?
- How we can solve the existing problem?
- Why is your city or region the best place to organize this meeting?
- Why is it time to organize this event in your region?

6. How?

Many organizers can have the best ideas, but if they will not answer how they are going to organize their event, it will be not realized. Therefore, you have to understand how you are going to organize your event.

With this point, you have to understand how you will be able to attract financial resources, people and target audiences. Do you attract sponsors or partners to help you to organize your event? Or finance yourself?

The questions to asks are:

- How many funding are available for organizations of the event?
- How can I involve sponsors and partners in the event to cover the costs?
- What would boost the main attraction of my event?
- What kind of cultural activities and food will add the value to the event?
- What is the business model of your event? How you will earn your income and benefits?

As you can see, there are many questions to ask. It means that the larger events need time and resources to plan and organize an event. From my experience, for the largest international event we were preparing 1 year. You need many resources and patience to realize your events. Be prepared for hard work.

As a practical part, let me show a sample table for defining the concept of an event below.

Table 1 Concept Ask Questions

Questions	Your Answers (*Sample draft below*)
What?	*Argentina International Economic Forum*
Where?	*Capital Congress Hall*
When?	*October 21-23*
Who?	*Political leaders, Economists, Investors, Businessmen, Researchers*
Why?	*To discuss key issues of the region*
How?	*In partnership with the Astana Economic Forum*

The table above is very simple and takes almost no time. In the second column, you should write your answers about your event.

Start your event preparation with table 1. And you will build your concept easily!

Usually the first concept is in two pages in word document or 6-7 slides in power point presentation. To illustrate let me, show you the concept of the III Astana Economic Forum. It was in the form of power point presentation, but here I copied the slides into word document.

Sample 1 The Concept of the Astana Economic Forum, 2010

Concept of the Astana Economic Forum, 2010

Event type: Forum

Name of Forum: Astana Economic Forum

Topic: Economic Growth Stabilization of Countries in Post-Crisis Period

Date: July 1-2, 2010

Mission: Discussion of conditions promoting long-term stable development of countries in post-crisis period

Goals:

- Working out formation mechanisms of conditions for promoting long-term stable development of world economy and countries in post-crisis period on the basis of consolidation of state economic policy, achievements of science and initiatives of private sector
- Assistance in the image development of the Republic of Kazakhstan as a rapid developing country with great potential for economic growth

Tasks:

- Discussion optimal economy structure in period of post-crisis development
- Creation conditions for shaping and developing new structure of stable, competitive economy.
- New concept of favorable investment climate for realization of innovative projects
- Discussion ways of creation new financial architecture, which will able to provide long-term and stable economic development
- Attraction of potential investors and partners into the innovative projects (exhibition of industrial-innovative projects)
- Exchange of practice and scientific developments between scientific schools of the world

Honored Guests:

- Marc Perrin de Brichambaut

Secretary General of the Organization for Security and Co-operation in Europe (OSCE)

- Finn E. Kydland

Norwegian Economist, Winner of the 2004 Nobel Prize in Economics "for his contribution to dynamic macroeconomics: the time consistency of economic policy and the driving forces behind business cycles"

- Yisrael Robert John Aumann

Israeli mathematician, professor of the Hebrew University of Jerusalem,
Winner of the 2005 Nobel Prize in Economics "for his work on conflict and cooperation through game-theory analysis"

- Robert A. Mundell

Canadian Economist, Winner of the 1999 Nobel Prize in Economics "for the creation of the international economic model and the theory of optimum currency areas which led to the creation of the euro"

- Muhammad Yunus

Professor of economics, winner of the Nobel Peace Prize for the efforts to create economic and social development from below (Bangladesh)

- Zhao Shaoyu

Vice President of Asian Development Bank

In the past Deputy General Manager of Export-import Bank of China, where took positions as a Chairman of Committee for asset management and attraction of investment, and Procurement Committee

Participants:

- Leading scientific organizations and renowned scholars
- Representatives of central and local governmental bodies
- International organizations
- Leaders of foreign and domestic companies
- Representatives of foreign and Kazakhstan Mass Media
- Representatives of innovative funds, associations, non-governmental organizations, etc.

Partners:

- St. Petersburg International Economic Forum
- World Bank
- World Economic Forum
- UN Economic Commission for Europe
- German Center for Technical Cooperation
- Islamic Development Bank
- ESCAP
- Turkish International Cooperation and Development Agency

Business Model

If you are organizing your event first time and without any support, you have to think about a business model of your event as a necessary step.

The business model of the event is a structure, which means how your event will operate, build processes and generate revenues. The last is the most vital for your success, as the event preparation takes time and resources. You have to earn your revenues to cover your costs and earn some money to move further.

There are many types of business models are now available, including digital business models, which become more popular.

In fact, with your purpose to organize an event, you can generate revenues from the following activities:

1) Selling Delegate Packages.
2) Providing Special Services, such as translation, business meetings and etc.
3) Selling Exhibition Areas with Booths or without.
4) Sponsorship packages. Advertising your sponsors in various sessions or online.
5) Partnership packages. For example, organization of sessions by interested institutions.
6) VIP services. For example, organizing guest meeting at the airport, providing lux rooms, lux cars, best seats for the dates of forum and others.
7) Publication Fees for your event journal.
8) Advertising businesses on your web-site.

Your business model should work well to let you achieve your event's goals. And you have to pay a close attention to your clients, who can generate for you the highest value.

Start your concept with your business model! Later, you have to include your business model solutions in the services, packages and via available tools.

Event Architecture

Many events are complex in its scale, number of sessions and areas of discussions. To see clearly the whole map of the event, it is better to draw an architecture.

Organizing Astana Economic Forum, a main international event of Kazakhstan, I used to draw an architecture every year. It helped me and all our staff, including our top decision makers, to evaluate the event and involve many state, public and private institutions.

Let me provide you with the architecture of one of the Astana Economic Forums as an example.

Table 2 Draft Architecture of the Astana Economic Forum, 2011

Mission	Discussion of terms, providing long-term stable development of the world economy and individual states, assistance for identification and strengthening of the role of the Republic of Kazakhstan in the international community.		
Trends	**Global Economy and Finance**	**Business and Investment**	**Society and Stable Development**
Objectives	- Organization of discussions and debates on actual themes of global economy and finance - Gathering of recommendations and resolutions for the G20 and its governments	- Promotion of business development, and international cooperation for attracting investment - Organization of business dialogue - Conclusion of contracts, agreements and memorandums	- Assistance in reducing social and economic and legal problems in the Republic of Kazakhstan - Support of state and public development programs

The table 2 was the first architecture I designed for the event with target audience of more than 1,500 participants. As you can see from the trends and objectives, it connects your event to the activities of many organizations.

The event's architectures can be global in scope and include many other sections with descriptions of trends, sessions and activities. You can check one in the Appendix 5 as the next example.

The one common feature of my architectures is a global approach. You can see many topics and sessions for different sectors, but all of them relate to the global issues.

The architecture usually easily comes with the concept. But many experienced organizers, they start first with program. Or after the architecture design, they start their program development. Anyway, let's go to see how to develop the event program.

Event Program

The program or the agenda is the most powerful of all content for the participants, partners and sponsors to join the event. It is time consuming and you have to update your program almost till the day of the forum.

An event program is a description of the event, which is going to take place at the appointed date. It contains: topic, date of the event, venue, sessions and their descriptions, key speakers etc. In some of programs, it includes brief descriptions of the sessions, a number of participants (if places are limited for the larger events) and organizers and partners to underline their role and motivate others.

Generally, the program of the event will help an organizer in planning, organizing and actually attracting of your target audiences. Let's see its role for different clients of your event.

For staff:

Your staff will understand what are the main sessions and what should be done in near future to meet the requirements of the program. They will know what needs to be done, when and how the sessions will run so that they all run on time.

In other words, your staff will be more motivated to focus on their sessions or activities to bring the highest outcome.

For participants:

Your participants, i.e. guests and delegates, will know the main topics of discussions, who will be the top speakers, when and where this will happen. Your program will stimulate your participants to make their final decisions on planning and organizing their participation.

Most of the participants decide based on the topic of event or keynote speakers, others want to meet top people and attend the specific sessions etc.

To attract international participants, you have to translate your program as soon as possible.

The earlier you publish your program, the earlier you will start selling your packages.

For suppliers:

Your suppliers will evaluate the time of your sessions and activities, so that they will offer you the best prices and appropriate services on time.

For partners and sponsors:

Your partners and sponsors will evaluate who is taking part as a speaker and partner, what are your sessions and activities about, so that they will be motivated to join your event and offer their services or funding opportunities.

Taking all this into account, let's try to make a program of the event.

Following you will find the best tips and strategies how to prepare your event program.

How to create a program for the event?

There are many ways to start creating your program of the event. There is no specific rule to make it creative and attractive. I recommend to start with an outline and a draft plan.

There are many ways to start your outlining. It is important to be creative, think about the topic and all the great people you can invite for your event.

To outline a major point, I usually use tables with two columns like below. You can call it as an event schedule.

Table 3 Draft Plan of the Event Program

Date/Time/Venue	Session/Activity
21 April	International Conference for Agriculture
10:00-10:30 Hall A	Opening Ceremony, Palace of Independence Seats: 300
10:30-12:00 Hall B	Session on Agricultural Industrial Complex Seats: 350
12:00-13:30 Hall B	Session on Agricultural Machinery Seats: 350
13:30-15:00 Hall A	Lunch Seats: 300
15:00-16:30 Hall A	Session on Agricultural Science and Technology Seats: 350
16:30-17:00 Hall A	Closing Ceremony Seats: 350

First, include main sessions like in the table. The final version of your table, you can save it as a schedule. Later you can use it for yourself by printing out and putting it on your wall.

Second, define dates, time and venue.

Your web-site's main program page will also need a short schedule, rather than a full program. So, scheduling is the first step to see a big picture of your event.

The next step, you can briefly describe your sessions and number of participants. If you have co-organizers and partners you can also add them at the bottom of the description.

Third, define key figures, it means moderators and speakers. First time you can place TBD status next to each moderator or speaker, (to be defined) until the moderator or speakers will confirm the participation.

Fourth, design your program accordingly. You can use your creative decorations, frames, fonts and colors.

Fifth, publish the program on your web-site, hand it to your staff, suppliers and partners. Your programs should be translated into several languages to be on the air.

Sixth, send your program as attachment with your letters of invitation to your potential participants.

You have to update your program constantly, especially if you organize the international event with participation of key confirmed speakers and moderators. You have to update your program in 3 languages till the date of the event.

Remember! always put a note in any document such as: "Last changed on Dec. 25, 2019". So that participants will understand that their version is old.

In this way, you can design and update any program of your event: family, business, public or an international event.

To provide you with a program example, let's check a sample program of the high-level meeting below.

Sample 2 The Program of the Meeting

THE PROGRAM OF MEETING

COMPANY: LINK INVEST CAPITAL

REPRESENTATIVE: MR. BENNY NG, CO-FOUNDER

CITY: SHYMKENT

DATE FOR MEETING: 2017-12-09

Time	Activities	Responsible	Venue
10:00-10:10	*Welcome word*	Kuanysh Baitore	RIC
10:10-10:20	*Introduction, Company Overview, Investor and Investment Portfolio*	Benny Ng	RIC
10:20-10:25	*Introduction of the Mining Project*	Benny Ng	RIC
10:25-10:30	*Discussion of Mining and Export projects of South Kazakhstan Region*	Kuanysh Baitore, Benny Ng, Tulkin Narmetov, Nurbek Achilov	RIC
10:30-10:40	*Signing Ceremony of Memorandum*	Benny Ng, Kuanysh Baitore	RIC
10:40-10:50	*Coffee-break*	Anel Asilova	RIC
11:30-12:30	*Meeting with Head of Kazakh-Invest Company*	Kuanysh Baitore	*(to be confirmed)*
13:00-14:30	*Lunch*	Anel Asilova	
15:00-16:00	*Meeting with Deputy of Mayor Mr. Baurzhan Zhamalov*	Kuanysh Baitore	Akimat of South-Kazakhstan region (to be confirmed)
16:00-17:00	Summary of Meetings	All	RIC

In addition, you can also check the program of the Astana Economic Forum in the Appendix 10. This is a shortcut version, however.

To design a program, you do not need special skills. As you see in the table above, any program should include time, activity, a responsible person and venue. However, let's see how we can improve the program development by strategies below.

To organize your event and make it a big success requires many efforts, resources and patience. I decided to provide you with some of my tips and strategies from my past experiences:

1. Start your program preparation as early as possible. Even for events, which you plan urgently start with the program preparation first.
2. Use excel sheet or tables to schedule your event. Make it step by step and see a clear picture of your event in your first step.
3. If you are out of time, please check out for ready templates from this book or on the internet. You can find many varieties of templates for program design. Use the one that best fits your style and topic.
4. In order to plan and define a venue, please understand your guests. If they are the first time in your country, you can show all the beauties of your city or country by organizing in the skyscraper of your city or in the national park near your city. Of course, this depends on the topic and many other issues. At least, you can include cultural program or excursion tour to outside of the city.
5. To define the date of the event, please check the calendar of your plans first and think about what is the best date in the year to organize this event in your country. If you plan your event in the comfortable season you will save nerves and money. Also, think about when the unique fruits and vegetables of the region are getting ready. Foreign guests will like to try them definitely.
6. To make your program topic shining and attractive, you have to check and think about main trends and issues around. You can ask also university professors or experts in your area for brainstorming or supporting your event.
7. To define the main participants of your program, for example moderators and speakers, you have to understand the level of your event. For international events, it is better to invite experts and top figures from global organizations. For regional events, you can invite regional leaders of business and politics or very well-known experts from other sectors. For company events, you can invite a well-known expert, based on your plans to start a project, resolve an issue or cover a new market segment. For family events, you can call the best and popular artists and singers from the region.
8. To select moderators and speakers, please make a separate list to invite them as early as possible. You have to receive confirmations and include them in the program. It will sound stronger when you send it with invitation letters or publish on your web-site.
9. In order to plan your event efficiently and if you do not know, who will appear in your event from the list of the guests, it is better to organize your registration system online, at least 6 months before the event day.
   Remember that many international experts plan their traveling at least 6 months before. Some of the experts need adaptation period or have to learn about the country and culture before they will arrive.
10. For bigger international events, you have to place your program of the event as soon as possible on your web-site and constantly update it.
11. In addition, for international events, you have to place your program in several languages.

12. Plan your program with Gala Dinners including exotic menus of your country, food and drinks, so that participants can relax and feel comfortable for networking and businesses after busy event day.
13. For the first visitors of your company, city or country, you can offer a specially designed cultural program with national music, drinks, food or clothes.
14. Make sure that you have planned enough time for session flows in the program, especially for those activities, which are in different venues and locations.
15. To make your program understandable for any type of reader and especially with global topics, please include a short description of each session in the program.
16. For key topics of your event, please include in the program the number of seats available in the session hall. So that your participants will understand of the importance of early registration.
17. For attracting additional partners or sponsors, you have to place the name and logo of your existing co-organizers and sponsors in each session of the program and on all pages of your web-sites.
18. Appoint your program manager to update your program constantly. This manager should constantly check updates from other colleagues and do changes. He or she should be able to translate the program in to required languages and place them further on your web-site.

Human Resources

We cannot imagine any event or activity without human participation.

Human Resources are a key element for successful organization and implementation of any event, starting from planning up until the last day of your report.

If you an organizer, you have to imagine all activities of the event and build a structure for your team participation.

They have to not only act as coordinators in the event organization, but also bring their personal characters, creativeness and unique contribution. For that, they have to understand their roles and opportunities for growth.

It is important to start discussing about all this in your HR hiring process. It will help you to select the professional staff, who will have a clear organizational structure, functions and their roles in your event.

But for you, as an organizer, it is important to build the organizational structure first. Let's try to see how we can do it.

Organizational Structure

Organizational structure is a chart or table that will allow you to see clearly the activities, team's role, information channels and responsible managers.

Having an organizational structure in place your team will be efficient and focused on achieving the main goal of the event.

Depending on your event scale, you can start first with outlining and drawing a draft organizational structure. Let's do it right now.

First, outline a list of activities of the event

You can do it by drawing a plain table in Excel sheet or word document like below. You have to insert entire list of activities in to this table.

Table 1 List of event activities

#	Activities
1.	HR management
2.	Hiring
3.	Training
4.	Research and Analysis
5.	Program Development
6.	Program Scheduling
7.	Opening and Closing Sessions
8.	Session Management
9.	VIP Guest Management
10.	Web-site Development
11.	IT Infrastructure
12.	Content Development

13.	Event Promotion and Advertising
14.	Marketing and PR
15.	Registration of the Guests, Participants
16.	Badge Printing
17.	Handouts Design and Printing
18.	Seat calculation and schedule
19.	Logistics Management: Airport Pickup, Hotel, Event Venue, Cultural Programs
20.	Transport Management
21.	Food and Meal Management
22.	Partners and Sponsors
23.	Online Promotion
24.	Cost Management
25.	Payment Management
26.	Other

Second, make a table with 3 columns: 1) Activities; 2) Full name of your team members; 3) Functions

It means, that after you added your activities, you have to define your staff role and their functions and responsibilities.

The number of staffs for each activity depend on the event scale. The bigger the event, the more staff you can allocate for certain activity. It depends also on priorities. For example, you can prioritize your advertising after your web-site is ready. Up until that time, you can prioritize on content work.

So, let's draw a table to see in practice. Fill out the table with your activities, functions and staff members. The names in the table below are fictional and used as a sample one.

Table 5 Draft Table for Building Organizational Structure

#	Activities	Full Name	Functions and Responsibilities
1	Team leader	Nigel	Management, Control and Motivation
2	Senior Event Manager for Content and Program	Brown	Content development, program development
3	Senior Event Manager for Organization and Information Activities	Nike	Organization, Information Support, Promotion, Advertising
4	Senior Event Manager for Logistics	Julia	Logistics, Transport, Tickets, Hotel, Meals
5	Senior Event Manager for Finance, Accounting and Staff	Alisher	Finance, Accounting, Payments, Cost Calculation, HR
6	Content Manager	Madina	Content Development
7	Program Manager	Steve	Program Development, Scheduling
8	Opening and Closing Manager	Mike	Organization of opening and closing

9	Session 1 Manager	Elena	Session Manager (for example, on Economic Development)
10	IT Manager	Harish	IT infrastructure Manager,
11	Web-site Administrator	Beck	Web-site Administration
12	Online Marketing Manager	Alice	Promotion and content in the internet and web-site
13	Marketing and PR Manager	Aida	Marketing, PR, Handouts, Promotion of the Event and Sponsors in Media and During Event, Cultural Activities
14	Manager for Partnerships	Nurbek	Partners and Sponsors
15	VIP Account Manager	Dinara	VIP Guests, Speakers and Moderators, Anchors etc.
16	Cost Manager	Amanda	Cost Calculation, Analysis and Approval
17	Payment Manager	Yuliya	Payments, Agreeing and Analysis
18	Logistics Manager	Alan	Airport, Hotel, Event Venue etc.
19	Food and Meal Manager	Benin	Food, Meals, Coffee-breaks: Scheduling and Organization
20	Transport Manager	Yarosh	Transport Control, Transport Schedule
21	HR Manager	Farida	Staff, Volunteers, Organizational Structure, Hiring, Training, Volunteers etc.

You can take all the data from your organization's legal or HR department. In some organization there is a staff list with full names, positions and salary level. Some organization might already have their organizational chart. You can use this information or take from there for sure. But if you are going to organize your event. You have to draw a separate organizational structure for your event. And most importantly, you have to allocate your staff based on their professional background and ability to contribute effectively for your event project.

Third, draw an organizational chart of the event

There are many ways to draw your chart. You can do it in a special program or software and you can do it in excel sheet as well.

The structure should be easily understandable and clear to all: management, staff, partners, suppliers and volunteers etc.

For bigger events, you have to take into account, many details and allocate functions in your organizational structure so that everyone understands who is responsible for implementation and who is responsible for control and management. Let's see the figure 1 as an example first.

You can see from the figure that the organizational chart for the event can be so complex. But as you go through it, you can understand it easily. You learn that in the chart everything becomes clear and you notice that all roles are allocated.

The roles, which are not allocated, you can mark with a different color. For example, in the figure 1 you can see that free functions or roles of the chart are colored in red. This means that top managers have to urgently find and fulfill the positions or allocate the role to available coordinators.

Another point is that the telephone numbers of the key staff and coordinators are added in the chart, so that it means that any partner and team member can contact them easily. Generally, anyone can call and ask any question from them, as well as point out main event's issues, which need to be solved or clarified.

Figure 1 Organizational Structure of the VI Astana Economic Forum

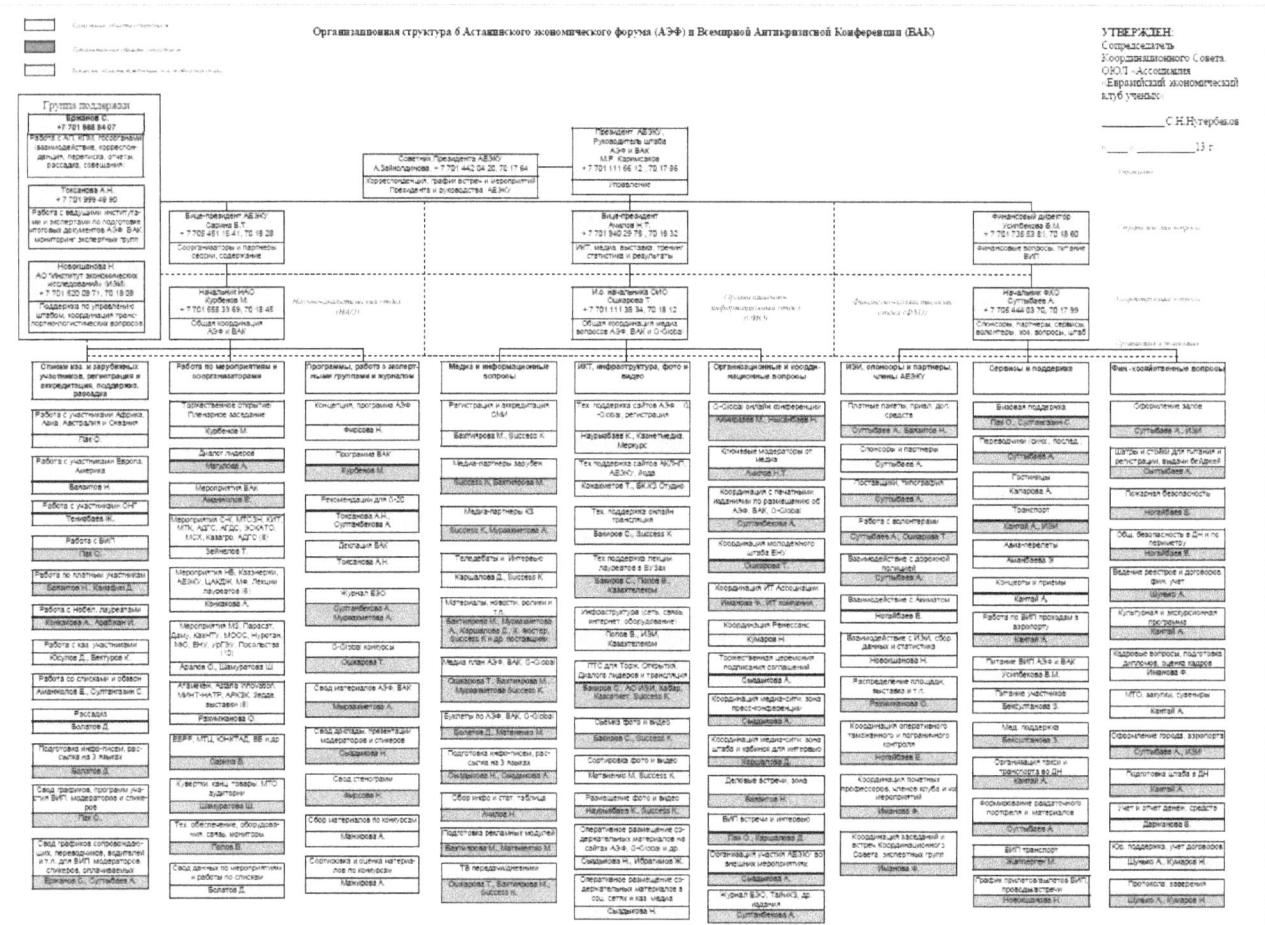

As a final step, your organizational chart should be approved by your top management before publishing. After it is agreed you can publish it on your web-site for information and as a contact source. You can further send it to all staff members for better coordination. Notably, for managers, who work in call-center or as web-site administrators.

Fourth, gradually update your chart

Update your organizational chart when you added new activities, telephone numbers or hired a new staff.

It is important to update your chart for effective communication and saving the time of your team, partners or participants.

Efficiency of Structure

We have demonstrated the organizational structure based on activities above.

Organizations, which want to organize events constantly can design an organizational structure appropriate to functions, divisions or multi-divisions. They can unite all forms of the organizational charts in one matrix structure as well.

No matter of a type of your organizational structure, it has to be clearly designed and benefit your organization, staff and clients in many ways.

Everyone should understand that it is not about putting a hierarchy to show who is a top and who is a lower manager, but mainly allocate your work force in order to play them a key role in achieving the event's goals. From my experience, the organized structure will strongly influence the income of the cadres and their professional growth. Because, your officers will be specialized in one activity, which nobody will do it better in the allocated time.

The structure also makes organization and its operations more efficient and result-oriented. All personnel will be responsible for their work and sector. It allows the event organizers to do multiple jobs and activities in parallel and in the most effective way. And if the link or sector works not so well, the management can also react quickly to train or replace the staff members.

You can also build your KPI System for HR to measure a performance of employees. KPIs of your HR helps organizations to achieve their goals by constantly analyzing the contribution of each team player. In most organization, implementation of KPI's fail, because organizations focus only on people's KPI, whereas they have to include processes, activities etc.

Anyway, your successful evaluation can be done by appropriate planning systems as well. Let's see how we can do it.

Event Planning

When you will have many years of true experience in organization of events, you become a professional. And you can see many elements which many new organizers do not take in to account, even with the best technologies in place.

For the experienced event organizer, a plan is the most important tool to control the preparation process and achieve the goals of the event. It helps also to grow your special monitoring skills and organize your thinking in the effective way to control the flow of your preparation.

Any plan is easier to do when you have a concept, program of the event and organizational chart. In addition, with an experience of organizing the events, it is much easier too.

Anyway, you can develop your plan without any difficulty by including all the details of the event's activities. This will provide you with the most effective preparation and organization of the event.

Generally, depending on time period, there are several types of plans which managers should develop to succeed in the event management. They are listed as follow:

1) Main Event Plan. This Plan outlines main activities for the whole period of the event management. For example, one year or two.
2) Action Plan. It includes main activities of each team member for one-month or a bigger period based on Main Event Plan.
3) Week Plan. Week goals are also important if you manage bigger events.
4) Day Plan. Each Manager has to organize a day to be efficient and achieve the goals step by step. It is important if you have limited budget, but want to organize a bigger event with a lot of activities or sessions.

In many teams, organizers omit week and day plans to be more productive and avoid spending too much time on writing plans and reports. But in this case, you have to organize short weekly and daily meetings at the beginning and at the end of the week for result checkups.

Let's start with Main Event Plan step by step.

Below is a table, where you can start with the main event planning. It takes no time for you if you know your staff and your main activities well. You have to check only about a calendar planning for defining your deadlines.

Table 6 Draft Main Event Plan

Month	Activities	Deadline	Responsible
January	Develop plans and action plans	15 January	Nick
February	Hire plan of staff and suppliers	5 February	Steve
March	Launch web-site for registration	8 March	Kathy
April	Develop content	1 April	Samir
May	Start promoting your event	1 May	Nigel
June	Start booking tickets, hotels etc.	15 June	Alice
July	Printouts, badges	15 July	Mike
August	Event Day	5 August	All
August-September	After-event promotion	15 September	Nigel

Above introduced plan is the first and easy outline to go further for details. Generally, in your event plan you can include more details depending on purposes of your event. Let me provide an illustration from my experience, when we designed the event plan for organization of the EXPO 2017 in Appendix 1.

We prepared this plan in the December 2016, around 5-6 months before the Astana EXPO-2017 to offer for a main organizer of the exhibition. From this offer, not all activities were accepted, but as team coordinator I was participated in the organization of the two events.

However, the action plan in Appendix 1 again is a general plan without details. Each of the accepted activities were implemented by designing a separate action plan with all details for organization of the approved events.

Remember, that each team member has to understand their plan of work clearly and fully to achieve the goals of the event. They have to develop for them with their own creativity and passion to contribute.

For example, marketing team has to have their own plan of actions. Web-site coordinator – its own plan for realizing the web-project etc.

Planning manager can unite all the plans of the team in one document and checkup for the progress and corrections periodically.

As a result, top management can see the outcomes of the planning as a statistical information or as a schedule to check whether the task finished or has some issue.

Another important factor to consider is about planning of processes. Your event management system will be complex and feeble with process planning. Let's clarify this new topic in the next section below.

Event Processes

Process Design is one of the key strategies for the organizers to achieve efficiency in realization, monitoring, cost saving etc. I learned this discipline in Germany while doing MBA. As a really new direction in the Central Asia and in many organizations, it is still not taken into account or primitive.

In organizations, where I organized many events, I introduced the process management concepts by designing various charts and schemes of processes, for example, you can check one in the Appendix 6. Many of my colleagues were asking me a lot of questions and some of them were thinking it is a waste of time. But, generally, after they saw the chart they were relaxed and wanted to know more. They were thanking me for clarity of work and goals. As you can see in Appendix 6, the scope of the activities and, at the same time, processes about how a participant moves from one stage to another are described in a coherent way.

The chart or scheme of processes help your team to image all the logic of the event and see where to concentrate efforts, resources.

Generally, a flowchart of processes in the Appendix 6 consists of 3 stages:

1) Preparatory Stage, which starts 9-12 months before the event.
2) Realization Stage, which starts 2-10 days before the event and last till the end.
3) Post Forum Stage, which last up to 6 months after the forum.

In each stage, you can see: the process blocks, web-infrastructure, organizer's activities and various activities with the participants.

From management point, it helps to see a blueprint of the event for decision making and action plans. When you see your whole process, activities and necessary infrastructure in one picture, as an organizer, you can see all the work, which should be completed in time and with the best quality. Your personnel can also understand the scope of planned work and do their contributions effectively.

The best tip is to make sure that you designed all activities of your event in one process chart, including marketing and sales activities.

Event Marketing

When everything in place, the first activity to start is marketing and media communication.

As an organizer, it is important to focus on marketing and promotion of the event from the first day of your preparation. Especially, if you are organizing your event for international audience.

The most important marketing activities and tools, to keep in mind, are:

1) Hire, involve and educate marketing team;
2) Do marketing research of major events for benchmarking and pricing;
3) Develop a web-site for marketing and registration;
4) Content development for your target groups;
5) Build relationships with your audiences via content, online forums or discussions;
6) Attract journalists and media;
7) Design your attractions of the event;
8) Prepare the printouts and materials;
9) Organize surveys of your target audiences etc.

For realization of marketing activities, you can use your separate plan of marketing and also you can design a detailed program based on marketing research.

If you do not know how to do it! Do not worry! This book will help you to give many ideas and prepare your best event organization in marketing and media.

First let me outline main marketing areas for your practical implementation.

Marketing research

Marketing Research is a necessary tool to understand the dynamics of your topic to effectively compete with many other events.

Based on marketing research and information, you can design a new marketing plan, business model, new package or new service for your participants.

CRM system

CRM system is an e-business tool that can help you to build your customer relationship of your event with all your clients, including sponsors, suppliers and partners in one single platform. It can organize all of your marketing and sales activities, including your emails, contacts, telephone communications, deals, and more.

For international events, you need your own CRM system as a must. There are many ready CRM systems are available online. You can set up one and adapt it to your event and needs.

Check some useful links for CRM platform at the end of this book too.

Promotion and advertising of the event

Promotion and advertising are a marketing communication tool which defines and promotes your event through media channels, search engines, social media or your web-resources.

For international and high level of events, you can plan a separate promotion and advertising campaign program to attract high level experts and leaders of politics, business etc.

Remember, for promotion and advertising in the international arena you have to understand the cultural differences. There are many special issues and relations toward color, numbers, language usage etc.

Brand building of the event

If you want to organize your event annually or periodically, you have to think about your event's brand. It is important to design and use your exclusive logo or trademark in all media and marketing content. It will bring about awareness of your specific event, while differentiating it from other annual international events.

Web-site

No matter how a massive event you are planning, it is important that you will design and launch a web-site. It is a key marketing tool to achieve a success for your event.

Generally, your web-site should contain the following sections:

- About Event
- Program
- Packages
- Participation package
- Exhibition
- Services
- Partners and Sponsors
- Contact information
- Useful Links

You have to fill out all sections with sound and attractive information. The pages have to be connected in logic and draw visitors for registration.

Your web-site is the first landing point of your potential participants. So, it means that it should be well-designed and should be understandable to use it for new information from any place around the world.

For lifetime participation, you can also create an online forum or blog section. All topics of the event can be described there for contribution. In this way, participants can discuss key issues of the event beforehand and have their time to prepare recommendations and resolutions of the event. This is very important for economic, social and ecological events.

Market Segmentation

Segmentation will help you to save your budget and time. If you have your concept and plan, it is much easier to define your segment, as you have already had it in your concept. But, if you do not have, you have to understand the main segments. Let's check them out and explain.

If you are organizing your family event, you will be interested to invite:

1) Family members

2) Friends
3) Colleagues
4) Neighbors
5) Popular artists or stars

If you are organizing your business event, you will be interested to invite:

1) Colleagues
2) Partners
3) Suppliers
4) Clients
5) Sponsors etc.

If you are organizing public or international event, for example in economic topics, you will be interested to invite:

1) Political leaders
2) International organizations
3) Nobel Laureates
4) Economists
5) Scientists and Academician
6) Businessmen
7) Experts and specialists
8) Investors
9) SME
10) Government organizations
11) Non-governmental sector
12) Media

Segmentation is dividing your market into the groups based on geographic, socio-economic, cultural, demographic etc. factors. It will help at the end to define your target niche in each group. And finally, it will serve your business model to reach more revenues.

Packages and Pricing

Event packages are generally your event's product. So, you have to pay the highest attention to your product development.

After a market research and segmentation, you can clearly see your target groups. As an organizer, you understand average salaries, age, interests, and the purchasing power of your niche.

Based on this information, you can design your event packages in the most effective way. So, the first question, how to design your package and define your pricing for packages.

Let's start with sample packages, which are presented in the Appendix 2 based on my experiences in the organization of the international event.

For packages, it is better to understand your services, which create an additional value for your potential participant. You have to think about them long before you start creating your packages. You can research the packages of other events and compare them with yours for various benefits, services and pricing.

The final stage of your package development is defining your pricing. It is a marketing process of defining a value of your packages in terms of cost. It can be based on costs, perceived value, comparative pricing, market prices and freemium.

For example, you can define prices based on perceived value of packages:

-Standard

-Economy

-Premium

You can also specify pricing based on association with the similar services in the market, for example:

-Gold

-Silver

-Bronze etc.

For bigger events, you can also practice functional pricing, for example:

-Transport Package. You can offer transport service companies for sponsorships.

-Session Package. You can offer specialized international and state organization, which are ready to organize a session within your event.

Anyway, you should analyze your market and use your creativity to build your services of the packages. And you have to use your marketing skills for price evaluation and comparison to define the most optimal one. At the end, your packages should not be higher than the packages of international events, which have long history and bigger influence. And it should not be very low if you want to attract investors and the best experts in field.

Event Promotion

When your program and packages are ready and, they are on your web-site, the next important step is promotion of your event.

There are many marketing strategies to start promoting your event. Marketing strategies are useful not only for promoting your event, but also for brand building, promotion of your country or city and also your personal image as well.

Here, in this section, I will try to advice you with the most common and popular marketing strategies and tips, taking into account my own experiences in the event organization.

Let's start with them.

Content creation

Almost all delegates and participants of the events, except for family events, make decision based on past experiences and available content about the event, its reviews and previous outcomes.

But if your event is a new one and you do not have any testimonials from participants, you better learn how to promote your event by creating a content about a topic, sessions, key speakers, moderators, attractions, cultural programs, your city, country etc.

Content development is the most important indicator of your quality. You can hire the specialists as well as freelancers for a period of the event preparation. The most important requirement is that your content should describe your intentions clearly and with creative approach that could lead a reader of your content for a thinking about your event. Better, for a decision making to participate in your event.

Make you positive effort for building an outstanding content development team.

Send your invitations by post and email

One of the perfect ways to invite participants is to send your emails if you know the email address or send it by post.

However, you can also automate sending your e-invitations by online systems such as www.mailchimp.com. Some of them you can find in the useful links at the end of the book.

Usually, it will take 1-2 weeks of waiting to receive an answer for your email. For example, if the person will be interested, he will register via the link you mentioned and write you a positive letter that he will participate in your event. He may also request additional information or services. You have to check your CRM to clarify what type of participant he is and take your actions to serve him.

If he will be busy with other activities, he will write you about this with pointing out on future possibilities. Don't ignore this letter, follow-up with the positive answer too. It might happen if the planned event will be postponed and he may decide to participate in your event.

There are participants, who will be asking a lot of questions and support in order to decide on registration or participation. Be open and supportive and you will get their confirmation. If he is a top-level participant, he will ask additional support definitely.

The most important part of emailing is to prepare mail lists. By name, position, organization, contacts etc.

It will take time to make a high-quality list. To prepare, you have to check the addresses and telephones. As in many cases, some of the information taken from databases or internet will be outdated.

One of the main mistakes is sending the same email to one person many times. So, it is important to use a CRM system or services like mailchimp.com.

After sending the first email, you can repeat your letter with a new motivating message to the same list in a week, but omitting those who have already registered or unsubscribed from your list.

Promotlon via a web-site

It is important to launch a web-site of the event with a sound name and logo as the first step. Any customer should find your web via search engines to learn your event packages, as well as program, services and other information.

In the web-site you can promote not only your event, but also your city and region. It is also the best way to introduce your touristic destinations in the cultural packages, for example.

Use social media for promotion

Using social pages will help your event become more popular by increasing your followers, potential participants, partners and suppliers. It will help you to promote key messages for your specific audiences in various market segments. For example, if you want to attract CEOs of the company from Europe, you can easily do it in the social media by targeting to Europe.

As you know, there are many types of Social Media. The most popular are Facebook, Twitter, LinkedIn, Instagram and YouTube. You can build your own plan for each of the social media for promotion and advertising.

For promotion, you can also use the book titled: "200 Websites and Tools for your Online Presences" by Nurbek Achilov. There are many useful links to promote your event in the internet.

Launch your online forum or blog

Many events are difficult to understand if your participants have never heard about specific terms and never interested in global economics or trends.

You can uncover such topics step by step and interest your target audiences via blogs. For example, an investor, you are interested in, could be from automobile industry. And, he would invest only in automobile business. At the same time, your topic is about global ecology, which can be so new topic for the investor. Therefore, you have to show how the investor can be useful for the world by investing in the projects for decreasing CO_2, for example, creating electric cars or special car filters and engines.

With online forum and blogs, you can attract your target groups step by step. They will be more than happy to support your events and use opportunities for discussions, investing and speaking.

Set up search engines for promotion

Every day millions of people search for their products and services online. SEO will help you to find your participants based on their interests easily. Keywords, tags, titles of your event will help your clients find your page effectively.

It is important to analyze and select your keywords and spend some time. The selected keywords have to increase a webpage's performance in web search results.

For better performance, you can create a daily budget for the best 7-10 keywords. By number of calls, emails and leads, you can control the budget increasing or decreasing it. Also changing keywords or target countries.

Create an affiliate program

Annual Investment Meeting's organizers in Dubai use affiliate program to let intermediate people earn around 15-20% from attracting delegates. In Astana Economic Forum, it was about 3-5% when I worked in the past.

It is a really great motivation. By selling your packages, your active partners can earn money, indeed. They will be motivated to share their views about your packages, links and advantages in their groups, countries etc. To implement, it is important to learn a whole value chain of the affiliate program. The first-rate program is the one, when you and your partners benefit from it, especially loyal partners.

PR

Building relations with public is the most important element not only for promotion, but also for relationship building and receiving supports.

In many cases, if you are not talking and communicating with your public, they will be reluctant and can quickly create a negative image about your event. Especially, if you try to connect your event with politicians, which made wrong decisions for communities. For example, many times I heard in media, that events are waste of state money, when millions of people live in poverty, or events are political instruments of the corrupted political leaders. Imagine a situation, if the half of the population believe in the word of mouth. So, your event can fail without any further interest for your target audience.

Therefore, public relations are another way of approaching to your audiences for creating a positive image about your event. If you do not know how to do it. You can always involve experienced journalists and media agencies.

Media Plan

Media planning is generally about attracting professional specialists and companies for your promotion. They can do all the job and services based on their experiences.

Media agencies, with a wide network of journalists and media agencies, are usually the best implementers of your media plan.

For small events, for example, family events, you can try with your own media plan.

For bigger and international events, media plan is a vital instrument to spread the voices of your event all around the country and beyond. Therefore, it is important to attract an experienced media agency if you do not have your own media team.

For any case, let me provide you with some of the strategies and show you how to outline the draft media plan.

First, start with your table creation as in the table 7.

Second, list all of the media you want to target.

Table 7 Draft Media List Preparation

Media	Name/Location	Media Content
Web-site	Event Web-site	Information, Analytics, Statistics, Program, Speakers etc.
Newspapers	Wall Street Journal, New York Times	Editorial, Columns, Articles, Ads
Magazines	Economists, Vox, International Monitor	Editorial, Columns, Articles, Ads
TV	CNBC, Bloomberg, BBC, CNN, Euronews etc.	Editorial Documentary, Ads, Interviews etc.
Social Media	Facebook, Twitter, Instagram, Youtube, etc.	Short Messages, Links, Infographics, Publications, Video, Ads, etc.
Search Engines	Google, Yandex, Yahoo, Rambler, Bing	Register your site, Select keywords for promotion, Ads

Blogs	Blogger.com, Wordpress etc.	Publish blogs, register Google AdSense
Billboards	Streets, Airport, Public places, Roads	Ads
Messengers	WhatsApp, Telegram, Viber, Skype, etc.	News, updates, links etc.

Third, insert media channels where you will promote.

Fourth, indicate main media content you will use for each media channel.

Fifth, create your media calendar with allocating all your media in the calendar. To see an example, please check Appendix 3. You have to allocate your media activities for pre-event, post-event and during event period.

Sixth, discuss and allocate staff, suppliers and partners to support your media plan realization. You or your media company has to compile a list of journalists and media for invitations and media partnerships.

Seventh, update your media plan for new partners, content types, channels etc.

With effective promotion and marketing campaign, you will receive many proposals for partnerships every day. Meet, discuss and communicate to confirm your media partnerships! Include them in the media plan and let this know to all of your team members by updating. That's for all now.

If everything goes according to the event's plans, including the media plan above, you will have no difficulties with your registration – a main stage of your first involvement with your participants.

Event Registration

The objective of all events is to register participants in your system to work further. It is a cornerstone of a revenue generation. Without registration you cannot meet your requirements of your costs, sponsors and your own sustainability.

If you have planned well, taking into account all aspects of the event organization, you will have no problem with the registration.

Usually, registration stage is the final stage of the decision-making of the participant. But you have to organize your logic of registration and the fields of registration in the most effective way to react instantly for information and any complain of your potential participants.

So, what are the important points to take into account in the event registration:

1) Registration Process

In the registration process, it is important to organize the logic of registration, which should lead a participant to the last stage, when a potential participant pay for the selected package.

If you organize an affiliate program with promo code and with special pricing, it will motivate your key partners, who can also benefit from registering participants.

Remember, your registration is the first experience of your potential participant with your product and it should be easy, understandable and without errors.

2) Registration Form

Registration form should be simple, with hints and not too long for adding information. You do not need to put all the fields in the first registration day of your potential participants. For example, you do not need to include visa questions. For visa support, a visa manager should know only a country of citizenship. So, after receiving a filled-out registration form from visa country, the manager should contact a participant and request to download a copy of the passport and fill out an additional visa application form in the personal page. In this situation, participants from visa free countries will not be contacted.

You should avoid forms where all participants, including those, who do not need visa, have to add their visa information. That's not accepted.

3) Participant Type

When you design your registration forms, it is important to categorize your registration fields of participants by type of participation. It will help organizers in communication with the registered delegates. You can also benefit from offering various services or partnerships depending on selected status of the registered participant.

In addition, categorization during your registration will help you in designing your access badges. Badges with different statuses will help you in managing flows during the forum. You can differentiate your participants easily in the venue. For example, you can organize a special area for media or VIP participants only. Or, media center can be accessible only for journalists.

From my own experience, we divided participants on the following types:

1) Participant
2) VIP
3) Media
4) Investor
5) Partner
6) Organizer

During registration process, a potential participant selects his own type of participation. If you know that a participant selected as VIP or Investor for participation – you can have a chance to offer additional services.

If you see that your participant is a media representative or a director of the media agency, you can talk about editorial article or media partnership.

For free events, you have to analyze your delegates accurately. You have to check many information and if required you can request information from the ministries of foreign affairs. For this, it is important to have a special manager.

4) CRM system

As mentioned previously, all registration should be recorded in the CRM system for effective operation with each of the participant.

With advanced CRM system, you can control:

- Emails;
- Calls;
- Requests;
- Notifications;
- New offers,
- New services
- Feedbacks
- Problems of participants etc.

With CRM in place, you can benefit in organizing your database in the most convenient way for your operation and activities.

5) Registration Support

If you have launched the web-site in 3 languages for registration. That's great!

But you can still have those participants, who will have problems with registration, because of language barrier or lack of computer and web-site skills.

There are countries in the world, where internet is still expensive or countries, where people do not speak neither English, nor a local language of your web-site.

For high quality services, it is important to organize for them registration support. It can be done online, via email or messengers.

6) Activities in the CRM System

With your database of participants in place, you have to work constantly on the following categorization:

a) Participants, who need visa support,
b) Participants, who need hotel booking,
c) Participants, who need airport pickup,
d) Participants, who need VIP status and services,
e) Participants, who want to make a speech or moderate if available,
f) Participants, who want to give interview to media,
g) Participants, who want to organize business meetings,
h) Participants, who want to register for cultural programs,
i) Participants, who want to submit their articles,
j) Participants, who want to do joint projects,
k) Participants, who want to invest in projects etc.

Effective operation in your database with your participants is the most important stage for increasing the outcome of your event many times. You can benefit from many new operations, activities and quality of services, provided in time and in the required standards.

Event Day

The final point of your preparation is an event day(-s). Indeed, some bigger events can last several days according to the schedule.

If you planned and completed all necessary preparation in time, your event should move smoothly and successfully. You have to coordinate only your staff for providing your services and supporting the delegates with the passion and high quality.

Moreover, the bigger events require special attention to the flow of sessions and participants. The following figure shows the sample employee distribution plan in order to control the flow of the participants in the first day of the forum.

Figure 2 Employee Distribution Plan

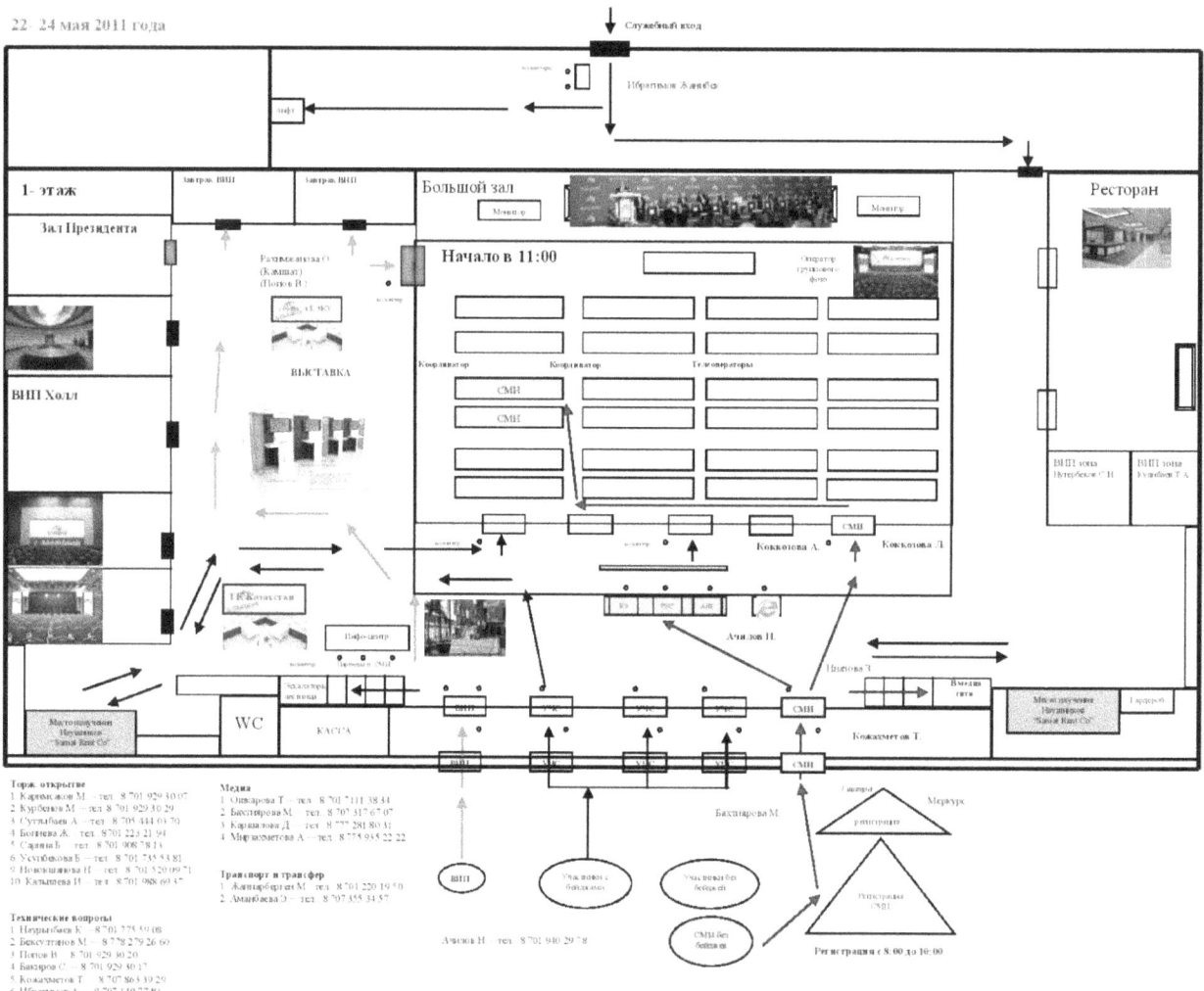

In the figure above, you can see the responsible areas of each coordinator and main corridors for flow of participants. With this scheme, you know your coordinators' location and flow of participants so that you can effectively control the whole chain of your event opening.

Generally, in order to increase the efficiency of your event day, you can apply the following tips and strategies:

1) Define the place and role of each staff member and volunteer in the venue and in online activities. A senior coordinator should check the coordinators and volunteers in their allocated place several hours before the opening of the event.

2) Put as many directions as possible in the venue to control your flow of participants, media, VIP etc. For many requests and support, you can organize an information center, located in the front of your main hall or the venue.

3) Make sure that participants receive notification in centralized way to be directed during the event. For example, in picking up badges, daily updates, about sessions, including the cultural programs etc. You can also launch a special mobile application for convenience.

4) For international events, you can organize printing of badges for participants of the events in many points, including at the airport or hotels. This will create a feeling of comfort and a positive mood about the organizers.

5) Badges should be printed out according to status of your participant such as participant, VIP, partner etc. It is recommended to mark the badges with different colors and chips to navigate your participants during the event and also for accessing the sessions or special areas.

6) You can organize the broadcasts from the sessions on YouTube, Facebook or on TV channels to reach bigger audiences. Make sure that you have reserved the traffic channels from local suppliers.

7) Your event day is an important day to gather feedbacks from your participants. You can organize it after the event, but you can do it during the event as well. Make sure that your feedback forms are printed out and placed in the convenient places. Or you can motivate the volunteers for a number of filled out feedback forms, which they have to gather from the participants.

8) The event day is a best time to advertise your sponsors and for taking pictures. Make sure that you prepared banners and video presentations for monitors with logos of partners and sponsors on them. You have to take some pictures and video with running video presentations or hanging banners for your sponsors. You have to do as many promotions of you sponsors as possible so that in the next event you will get their support easily.

9) Make sure that your coordinators check the session rooms for participants and announce the starting time of the session via microphone before they start. The best strategy, however, to design the seating arrangement of your session. It will help you learn about your participants of the session, and also you will be able to control the seats. If you design the seating arrangement electronically, that's even better. You can sell your seats providing an option for participants. For information, please check out the Appendix 8, where you can find the seating arrangement of the IV Astana Economic Forum by name of participants. It was done one by one, which makes it difficult to change. Now there are many available software, where you can do it electronically.

10) Make sure that coordinators control the change of nameplates, glasses and water on the tables of the speakers and moderators, especially, the consecutive sessions in row without breaks.

11) Control your media partners for content generation of your event.

12) Your content managers can publish photos, videos, and other messages in multiple social networks. This will allow to reach bigger audiences online.

13) One of your coordinators should control your photographers and video cameramen for best records and shots. In addition, they have to download all the records in one server periodically.

Make sure that your IT manager organized a special server for it, which will be accessible for your content managers.

14) Many speakers and moderators are busy people. They usually have to fly back in the same day. You have to serve them well so that next time they will be glad to join again.

15) For international events, please check out your meal menu for special dishes, particularly, for international VIP guests. For example, Muslim people do not eat pork, Indian – cow meat etc.

16) Control the logistics manager for transport schedules and drivers. Many high-ranking international delegates will be hurrying to the airport or hotel to catch their flights, so you have to provide their cars or buses in time.

17) Appoint key manager for volunteers to provide control for early substitutions. Managers or volunteers who work on the frontiers or with many requests require early substitutions every 3-4 hour to be effective. If more, it can create stressful situations for them and for participants.

18) Your content managers should be active to distribute handouts and promotional materials of the forum. The more materials you provide with your participants, the more changes that they will read your materials and see your unique information.

19) If you start early, you will not have difficulty with organizing interviews for top delegates of your event. Make sure that your interview kit with schedules is handed to all selected participants and journalists. So, everyone knows the time, room for own interview. During these interviews, journalists can also gather testimonials about the event for you.

20) Control the meeting flows. In the event area, you have to plan free wi-fi areas with comfortable chairs and sofas for chatting, networking and discussions. It is a good way to benefit your multiple participants, especially, if you did not plan special meetings for them.

After Event

Many organizers decide to relax after the event date. But this is wrong strategy. Because most of the participants will be still under impressions and your sponsors want to know the outcome and effects of their support right after the event. So, you have to focus on many issues after the event to be successful in future.

The following points are the tips and steps to improve after event activities.

1. Gather your statistics from coordinators, partners, sponsors, suppliers and all other contributors. As a final step, you have to prepare a report based on gathered data, statistics and feedbacks.
2. Send to all participants thank you letters. To motivate them, you can point out about the topic of the next event and ask them to participate, for example, in the online forum.
3. You can send, at the same time, electronic feedback form for your event evaluation.
4. Download all of your materials (videos, photos, publications, testimonials) on your web-sites. Inform by email your participants and ask them to share with friends, relatives and colleagues.
5. Publish them also in the social pages.
6. Calculate your costs and revenues. You have to understand how successful was your event, especially the first time.
7. Review your plans and outcomes of each employee.
8. Motivate the best contributors with bonus payments. During our events, we payed bonuses up 10 times more than the salary of the employee.
9. Review your supplier's contribution and calculate their cost and thank them for support.
10. Review your sponsors' and partners' contribution and personally thank them. Send them also the reports about the effects of partnership and their promotion.
11. Review your media partners' contribution and personally thank your journalists.
12. Provide the most hardworking employees with the certificates of acknowledgement.
13. Promote the final outcomes of your event, particularly of the global importance, in other international events and media channels. Make a plan of promotion beforehand.
14. Advertise main outcomes of the event in media and social networks.

For effective after event activities, it is important to have an action plan for follow-up activities with your all partners, sponsors and participants.

Report

Report writing is a final stage of your work. But it is so important as a planning of your event. That's because you have to present your reports to partners, sponsors, participants etc.

If you are planning a long-term event organization – report planning is a key for your long-term success.

Therefore, there are many outcomes to take into consideration for your report after your event. For example, you can explain in your report the outcomes in the terms of the following:

- Main ideas and outcomes of sessions, for example, resolutions or recommendations.
- Number of key participants: VIP, speakers, moderators etc.
- Number of participants, including international delegates;
- Number of journalists and their contribution;
- Number of sessions, sub-sessions, outside events;
- Number of testimonials;
- Photos;
- Video streams;
- Online Lectures of Nobel Laureates;
- Interviews of key participants;
- Number of media participants;
- Number of news, publications in media;
- Number of meetings;
- Number of contracts and MoU etc.

You have to include your indicators and statistics before event (i.e. plans) and after event (i.e. facts). Comparing them, you can see where you did progress and where you did not achieve it. So you can write about your perspectives to do it better event in the future.

How to write an effective report?

The following are the tips and steps for your finest outcome in writing your report:

1) Think about the report, structure it before the event date.
2) Prepare forms to gather statistics from your employees, partners, sponsors etc. They have to be adapted for each particular coordinator. You can see the general table of the statistics of the Astana Economic Forum in the Appendix 9. I was responsible for coordination of this general table for top management.
3) After the event day, gather your forms and statistics from all coordinators. You can check the sample statistics in the Appendix 4: The Outcome of the VI Astana Economic Forum and World Anti-Crisis Conference.
4) Your statistics is a preliminary statistic for your report writing.
5) Outline your report.
6) Make descriptions of each section.
7) Review files of your coordinators.
8) Compile your report.
9) Prepare the first draft of your report.

10) Review the report with your colleagues.

11) Include your feedback results.

12) Add your recommendations for organization of the next event.

13) Make final changes.

14) Prepare a power point presentation for your management, sponsors and partners.

15) Present your reports to your team, management, partners and sponsors.

Why do you need to write your event reports?

It is important that your sponsors, partners, suppliers and participants see the outcomes. Next time, if you decide to organize an annual event, they will be glad to join your event. The report of outcomes is one of the strongest elements for decision making and long-term cooperation with your clients.

How to get funding for your event?

New event organizers have many questions regarding attraction of funding.

Actually, there is no simple answer. It depends on many factors, including who are involved in your event organization.

However, many financial opportunities are available in the market for event organizers. They offer their funding with certain requirements and purposes to reach.

Let me list the strategies and tips to succeed in attracting funding.

1) Check out for funding from international organizations. Go through the web-sites of the international organizations first. Check the projects they are funding at the moment.
Many international organizations provide financial support based on the topic of event, location and many other specific issues.

2) Many non-governmental organizations are constantly organizing country specific events in different parts of the world. Check their web-sites out for their plans, especially for your country. Approach them and offer your ideas.

3) Attract private funds. Many business people are interested in promotion of their products, especially for export. So, offer them a special contract to support their business via events! They will be glad to join as partners of your event, at least. You have to do your best to find the optimal contribution structure for them.

4) Sponsorship packages. Make your sponsorship packages available as soon as possible. After you design and confirm your pricing, contact the largest companies of your region for sponsorship meetings. Present them your concept, plans and packages and future benefits for the sponsor. The chances are 10-30%, but you can improve it year after year, depending on your skills and topics of the events.

5) Attract Government. Many events benefit the economy of the city, region and even the country. It is one of the main sources of attracting the high-income tourists to the country. Therefore, prepare your plan of benefit for your local governors and talk to them for their support and funding.

6) There are many local and international organizations are on the way of organizing many forums, exhibitions, round tables etc. You can design your plan and cooperate with them for funding or sharing your costs.

7) Many universities and research centers organize their forums, conferences and events. You can design your plan to approach them and see perspectives for funding or sharing the costs.

Tips for partnership

Involving partners in event management and organization is a key for success. You have to understand that it is impossible to manage all the work by one person or organization. For international events, partnership is one way to make your event successful.

So, creating partnership is a hard work and takes efforts, time and understanding many factors of your work activities. In addition, you partners can become your sponsors if handled in the appropriate way.

There are some tips for event organizers I would like to share. They will help you how to find, attract and involve your partners, who are professional, successful and responsible. Let's check them out below:

1) Understand your event's mission, goals and tasks, as well as activities. You have to evaluate in which tasks or activities you are the best player and where you are not. You have to focus on the strongest sides of your team. Other activities you can outsource for your suppliers or attract a reliable partner.

2) You have to evaluate the benefits of your event and understand how you can share it with your partners? In which proportion?

3) Analyze your list of clients, partners, friends and discuss with them about partnerships. If they find a value for their companies, they will agree to join your event and support you.

4) Analyze the list of companies in the market. Evaluate which are the best at the functions and activities required for your event. Contact them. Share your goals and tasks. Define the roles and benefits for the partners. If they will agree, you are the best negotiator. If not, communicate step by step.

5) Analyze the list of state companies and governments. Evaluate how they can help you to organize your event. For example, to speed up the visa issue, provide additional security, or funding. Share your goals and tasks. Define the roles and benefits.

6) For long term partnership, you have to be clear, communicate regularly and respect your partners' ideas and proposals. Your partners have to understand a long-term effect of their contribution. For example, in Appendix 7 you can see one of the main charts, which we demonstrated to our main partner of the event.

7) As a necessary step, you have to sign MoU and a plan the actions to start activities for achieving the mutually beneficial goals. By putting every action in writing you will show your responsibility and eagerness to achieve the goals.

8) Partners are supporters. And you have to support them as well. You have to understand how you can support your partners in return to their support.

9) Your partners have to understand the benefits. If they will be frustrated by the amount of responsibility or work, remind your partners about the final benefits.

10) Organize open meetings with your partners and discuss with them key issues for support.

11) Provide your all partners with VIP status badges for participation, including in exclusive sessions of the event.

12) Allow your partners to register new participants under an affiliate program.

13) Invite partners to participate in the special VIP sessions during the event.

14) Include the logo of your partners in all media materials and handouts.

15) Place their logo on your marketing tools, including web-site and other pages.

16) Mention you partners during the speeches and interviews, articles and information materials.

17) Write about your partners in news and in your web-sites.

18) Praise your partners with certificates and thank you letters after the event.

19) Follow up with your partners on future plans and events.

20) Share your news and reports with your partners.

21) Keep in touch with your partners once in a month.

Useful Links

Here, you can find useful links for your event management activities.

CRM Systems

1) Zoho.com

Zoho is a web-based online office suite containing word processing, spreadsheets, presentations, databases, note-taking, wikis, web conferencing, customer relationship management, project management, invoicing, and other applications developed by ZOHO Corporation, a California-based company. Wikipedia.

2) SugarCRM

SugarCRM is a software company based in Cupertino, California. It produces the web application Sugar, a customer relationship management system. SugarCRM's functionality includes sales-force automation, marketing campaigns, customer support, collaboration, Mobile CRM, Social CRM and reporting. Wikipedia.

3) HubSpot

HubSpot is a developer and marketer of software products for inbound marketing and sales. Its products and services aim to provide tools for social media marketing, content management, web analytics and search engine optimization. Wikipedia.

4) Bitrix24

CRM Bitrix24 is a free social enterprise platform. It provides a platform to organize and track interaction with potential or existing clients, partners, agents and other contacts.

5) Agile CRM

Agile CRM is the world's first fully integrated sales, marketing and service suite – an All-in-One CRM for small businesses with full sales, marketing and service automation functionality.

6) SendinBlue

SendinBlue is a SaaS solution for relationship marketing. The company was founded in 2012 by Armand Thiberge and Kapil Sharma and offers a cloud-based email marketing/marketing automation SaaS suite that allows organizations to communicate directly with clients by email or SMS. Wikipedia.

Online Surveys and Mailing

7) Google Forms

Google Forms is a survey administration app that is included in the Google Drive office suite along with Google Docs, Google Sheets, and Google Slides. Forms features all of the collaboration and sharing features found in Docs, Sheets, and Slides. Wikipedia.

8) Mailchimp

Mailchimp is a marketing automation platform and an email marketing service. Wikipedia.

9) Survey Monkey

SurveyMonkey is an online survey development cloud-based software as a service company. Wikipedia.

10) Mailjet

The email platform for teams to send transactional & marketing emails.

Online News and PR

1) PR Newswire

PR Newswire network reaches nearly 3,000 newsrooms, like The New York Times, ABC News, BuzzFeed and more. They send content to over 550 news content systems like Moody's, SmartBriefs, LexisNexis and McGraw-Hill. PR Newswire's network reaches more than 4,500 U.S. websites, including popular sites such as Yahoo Finance, MarketWatch and Business Journals. Their global network reaches nearly 10,000 websites, portals and databases.

2) Business Wire

For more than 50 years, Business Wire has been the global leader in press release distribution and regulatory disclosure.

3) Investis Digital

Investis Digital is an international, digital corporate communications company, working with nearly 2,000 public companies in over 30 countries. Wikipedia.

4) PR Wire

As well as being a destination in its own right, PR Wire releases are fed into the ITJourno and Journo.com.au websites used by hundreds of journalists in Australia.

5) PR Distribution

Press Release Jet is the leader in press release distribution with the highest return on investment and lowest plan rates in the industry.

6) EIN Press Wire

EIN Presswire's distribution footprint reaches millions and combines a press release distribution service with media monitoring and RSS feeds that are used world-wide by journalists, professionals and businesses.

7) PR Web

For over 20 years, PRWeb has helped thousands of companies boost online awareness, drive website traffic and reach new customers. It's a proven, affordable way to impact your bottom-line.

8) Global Newswire

GlobeNewswire provides press release distribution services globally, with substantial operations in North America and Europe. Wikipedia.

Event Management Platforms

1) Whova

Whova enables you to manage your event from beginning to end within one system. It provides flexibility to opt in/out certain functionalities according to your needs (e.g. logistic management tools, conference management software, attendee and exhibitor engagement solutions).

2) Eventbrite

It is a popular ticketing solution for all kinds of events ranging from small meetups to large concerts. The system is customizable and allows people to register from their phones. You can use it to send email confirmations and reminders. They charge an extra 2.5% of the ticket price plus $1.99 per ticket and you can pass this fee onto the ticket buyers.

3) Cvent

Cvent provides software and services for event management such as venue sourcing, housing, traveling, online registration, etc. Their venue search option is useful, but it is limited to hotels. It's a good option for high-end events where the cost is less of a concern.

4) Trello

It is a project management software. If you're into the "to-do" "doing" and "done" task management approach, you'll love Trello. It has a strong visual interface, simple usability, and collaboration features for event management.

List of Event Management Software

5) Capterra

https://www.capterra.com/event-management-software/

Conclusion

You can definitely become the best event organizer one day. My advice - learn planning, follow tips and don't give up.

Every day there are thousands of opportunities to organize events. This is the way how we can develop ourselves and develop others. We have many issues to talk, discuss and find solutions for them. Get prepared, learn how to classify your event and define your target niche.

I am recommending this book for anyone who want to start the event organization. You can find many valuable tips and strategies how to make your event a very successful.

And for sure, I am here to answer any question you might have difficulty to do yourself. Please write me or email me if you need a support in event management and what applications you are using to share with me.

Wish you all the best!

About author

Nigel Aksel is a marketing specialist with more than 9 years of experience in event management, marketing, online activities and promotion. He is involved as a lecturer of marketing and project management at the South-Kazakhstan State University.

Nigel is a founder of several organizations and projects in several countries. He enjoys writing about multiple issues of university life, education and science. As a member of educational institutions, he understands well about the problems of education and science in CIS countries. He knows many areas of management and strategies how to improve the situation to help the local universities to adapt to the international level.

Appendix

FOR Y2016

AREAS: Sustainable Energy, Green Growth, EXPO-2017, Climate Change

Draft: 29.12.2015

№	ACTIVITIES	Form of completion	Execution	Deadlines	Scope (participants)	Additional information
9 ASTANA ECONOMIC FORUM						
1	Organization of forum and exhibition on topics of EXPO-2017 "Future Energy" in the frame of 9 Astana Economic Forum: Topics - EXPO-source of sustainable energy for all - Mini-EXPO-2017 Exhibition - International Climate Summit - Contribution of women to EXPO-2017	Report about forums and exhibitions, photo, video, recommendations, list of delegates, experts	Secretariat, EECSA, Coalition, EXPO&WOMEN, AVK	25-26 May	3 000	Total:
2	Creation of sustainable development committee and fund of the International Secretariat of G-Global with	Minutes of Meeting, List of committee members	Secretariat, EECSA	25-26 May	50	Organization of the first call within 9 AEF

	appointing coordinators to work with UN, international organizations and etc.				
3	Creation of Center of Green Technologies and Investment under the auspices of UN and organization of Press-conference	Minutes of Meeting, List of experts	Secretariat, EECSA	25-26 May	1 000	Initiative: "Sustainable Energy for All"
4	Ceremony of Signing of MoU between JSC "NC "Astana EXPO-2017" and interested parties	MoU, Action plan	Secretariat, EECSA	25-26 May	50	
	Total for Section				**4 100**	

ORGANIZATIONAL ACTIVITIES

5	Creation of 4 experts groups on 4 direction of EXPO-2017	Minutes of Meeting, Lists of members and experts	Secretariat, EECSA	January-March	100	
6	Organization of video production, preparation of banners, booklets and other information materials of Secretariat and EECSA with the purpose to distribute in	Photo, TV sport, Video film, Banners, Reports, Links and etc.	Secretariat, EECSA	January-December	5 000 000	

	the media, universities, scientific, research and business centers, web-portals					
7	Organization of online conferences on 4 topics of EXPO-2017: organization, trainings and technical support of participants	Video report, event report	Secretariat, EECSA	January-December	500	Total: 16 online conferences
8	Organization of business events and meetings with the purpose to attract companies, investors, experts and projects on topics of EXPO-2017	List of participants, investors, projects, experts and etc.	Secretariat, EECSA	January-December	10 000	Once in a month
9	Organization of meetings and round tables for launching 100 activities of EXPO-2017	Minutes, List of 100 activities for EXPO-2017, Action plan	Secretariat, EECSA	February-March	500	
10	Organization and creation of expert team for preparation of content documentation and materials of EXPO-2017 (articles, news, recommendations, etc)	Recommendation, Expert list News, Articles	Secretariat, EECSA	February-March	100	

11	Organization of round table on EXPO-2017 with the purpose to gather articles, infographics and analytical documents	Reports, Links, Materials	Secretariat, EECSA	February -March	1 000 000	
12	Organization of presentation and training for development of projects and business start-ups on topics of EXPO-2017 "Future Energy"	Links Presentations Start-up projects	Secretariat, EECSA	February -April	100	
13	Organization of meeting for development of EXPO-2017 and its promotion in media, among NGO and research centers	Report List of partners	Secretariat, EECSA	March-December	700 000	Involve journalists from database of 700K journalists and internet audience, involve members of EECSA
14	Organization of tour (including moto or bike) around 50 countries of Europe, Asia, America, Africa and CIS for promotion of EXPO-2017, signing MoU, inviting universities,	Photo report, MoU, Report on meetings, List of partners and participants	Secretariat, EECSA	May-October	50 000	Total: 8 trips

	international organizations, businesses, research and educational institutions				
	Total for Section				**6 762 800**	

SUSTAINABLE DEVELOPMENT AND GREEN ECONOMY

15	Implementation of the republican campaigns "Support the EXPO-2017" (Mini Expo, roundtables in 15 cities)	Report of campaigns, photo, video, list of participants, testimonials	Secretariat Coalition	January-December	15 000	
16	Create demo areas with the installation of renewable energy, followed by replication to other areas (urban and rural)	Report of campaigns, photo, video, list of participants, testimonials	Secretariat Coalition	March-August	100 000	
17	Organization of an international conference "Green Bridge Partnership Programme"	Report of campaigns, photo, video, list of participants, recommendations	Secretariat Coalition	November	400	
18	The launch of online competition EXPO-2017	Report of campaigns, photo, video, list of participants, list of jury, list of winners	Secretariat Coalition	January-November	10 000	
19	Organization of study tours: "EXPO-2017-a platform for energy efficiency and	Report of campaigns, photo, video, list of participants,	Secretariat Coalition	February-December	700	

	alternative energy sources" within the National Academy of Green Technologies"	recommendations				
	Total for Section				**126 100**	

YOUTH AND EXPO-2017

20	V International Economic Forum of Youth - "Energy of Youth"	Report of campaigns, photo, video, list of participants, testimonials	Secretariat AVK	May	1 000	
21	II International Green Bridge Youth Forum	Report of campaigns, photo, video, list of participants, testimonials	Secretariat AVK	October	1 500	
22	Gathering of the International Movement "Youth for EXPO" - EXPO Volunteers Forum	Report of campaigns, photo, video, list of participants, recommendations	Secretariat AVK	December	4 500	
23	II International Kazakh Waltz Ball (big ball in the open air)	Report of campaigns, photo, video, list of participants, recommendations	Secretariat AVK	July	1 500	
24	Motivational mcctings with university students on topic: "Energy of the Future"	Report of campaigns, photo, video, list of participants, recommendations	Secretariat AVK	January-December	5 000	

25	Monthly intellectual conference "PechaKucha Night Astana"	Report of campaigns, photo, video, list of participants, recommendations	Secretariat AVK	January-December	10 000	
26	Competition of green projects: "Green City"	Report of campaigns, photo, video, list of participants, list of jury, list of winners	Secretariat AVK	January-December	5 000	
27	The contest for start-ups: "Startup in Aul (Country Area)"	Report of campaigns, photo, video, list of participants, list of jury, list of winners	Secretariat AVK	January-December	5 000	
28	Republican campaign "My Country - My EXPO"	Report of campaigns, photo, video, list of participants, testimonials	Secretariat AVK	January-December	5 000	
29	Music Festival "Greenfest" (open-air)	Report of campaigns, photo, video, list of participants, testimonials	Secretariat AVK	June	2 000	
30	Exhibition of green innovations: "Green Future"	Report of campaigns, photo, video, list of participants, list of projects	Secretariat AVK	April	2 500	
31	International Conference TED EXPO	Report of campaigns, photo, video, list of participants, list of projects	Secretariat AVK	August	500	
32	Art Competition and	Report of campaigns, photo, video,	Secretariat AVK	May	1 500	

	Exhibition: "Sustainable Energy For All"	list of participants, list of projects			
33	Participation of supervisors and volunteers of EXPO 2017 in Antalya Expo 2016	Report of campaigns, photo, video, list of participants, recommendations for EXPO-2017	Secretariat AVK	August	150
34	Participation of supervisors and volunteers EXPO 2017 as volunteers at the Olympic Games in Rio de Janeiro	Report of campaigns, photo, video, list of participants, recommendations for EXPO-2017	Secretariat AVK	August	150
35	Participation of supervisors and volunteers EXPO 2017 as volunteers at the European Championship in France	Report of campaigns, photo, video, list of participants, recommendations for EXPO-2017	Secretariat AVK	June-July	150
36	Republican sports contest: "Energy of Youth"	Report of campaigns, photo, video, list of participants	Secretariat AVK	June	6 000
37	Online training of volunteers in Kazakhstan	Report of campaigns, photo, video, list of participants	Secretariat AVK	January-December	150 000
38	Youth Movie Festival "Kinomix"	Report of campaigns, photo, video, list of participants	Secretariat AVK	July	1 000
	Total for Section				**202 450**
WOMEN & EXPO-2017					

39	National industry award in the field of tourism	Report of campaigns, photo, video, list of participants, list of winners	Secretariat EXPO&WOMEN	March-November	800 000	
40	Business Women's Forum "Women's contribution to EXPO 2017" in the framework of 9 Astana Economic Forum	Report of campaigns, photo, video, list of participants, recommendations	Secretariat EXPO&WOMEN	25-26 May	150	
41	The Second International Forum: "Energy of the Future: Women, Business and the global economy" in Antalya, Turkey	Report of campaigns, photo, video, list of participants, recommendations	Secretariat EXPO&WOMEN	June	500	
42	International competition of TV spots: «My planet - my home».	Report of campaigns, photo, video, list of participants, jury and winners	Secretariat EXPO&WOMEN	April-October	200	
43	International festival of children's films	Report of campaigns, photo, video, list of participants, jury and winners	Secretariat EXPO&WOMEN	February-July	300 000	
44	Republican competition among domestic producers "Ulttyk Sapa" with awarding	Report of campaigns, photo, video, list of participants, jury and winners	Secretariat EXPO&WOMEN	January-October	500 000	

	a sign of "Recommended by EXPO-2017"				
45	Project: "ExpoSheber". Production of high quality souvenirs for EXPO-2017	Report of campaigns, photo, video, list of participants, jury and winners	Secretariat EXPO&WOMEN	January-December	100 000
46	Photo exhibition: "Legendary Women" Great Steppe"	Report of campaigns, photo, video, list of participants, jury and winners	Secretariat EXPO&WOMEN	March-December	150
47	Innovation Competition and startups of women	Report of campaigns, photo, video, list of participants, jury and winners	Secretariat EXPO&WOMEN	April-December	200
48	The Republican contest for Women's Initiatives: "Kazakhstan - energy future."	Report of campaigns, photo, video, list of participants, jury and winners	Secretariat EXPO&WOMEN	February-August	200
49	Competition of the world famous photographers to EXPO 2017: "Kazakhstan in my view"	Report of campaigns, photo, video, list of participants, jury and winners	Secretariat EXPO&WOMEN	May-September	50
50	Project: "The Bed and Breakfast: Green family village».	Report of campaigns, photo, video, list of participants, jury and winners	Secretariat EXPO&WOMEN	April-September	20
	Total for Section				**1 701 470**

	TOTAL FOR ALL SECTIONS			8 795 920	

Notes: abbreviations:

Exhibition – International exhibition EXPO-2017

Secretariat – International Secretariat G-Global

EECSA – Eurasian Economic Club of Scientists Association

Coalition – Coalition for "Green" Economy and G-Global Development

AVK – Alliance of Volunteers of Kazakhstan

EXPO-WOMEN – International Organization «EXPO &WOMEN»

№	Benefits	PREMIUM	BUSINESS	STANDARD
1.	Arrival/departure through the VIP/CIP terminals	yes	yes	-
2.	Discount for booking a hotel room for the Forum*	yes	yes	Up to 10 percent discount when circumstances allow
3.	Transportation from the Astana airport to the hotel and back	Premium-class car	Economy-class car	Group transportation by buses or vans
4.	Personal car from the hotel to the Forum to a lunch location and back to the hotel	yes	-	-
5.	Personal translator/assistant if needed	yes	-	-
6.	VIP entry to the Forum (a separate door and speedy registration)	yes	yes	-
7.	Information about your company on the Forum Web site (logo and description of the company's business)	yes	-	-
8.	Coffee breaks during the Forum	yes	yes	yes
9.	Access to two special dinners organized by the government of Kazakhstan	yes	yes	-
10.	Scheduling of a private meeting with one or more Forum participants, with room provided	yes	-	-
11.	Front-row seats at the Forum's opening and plenary session	yes	-	-
12.	Access to special-invitation sessions such as the Leaders Dialogue on new financial and economic policy	yes	yes	-
13.	Individual or group tour of Astana	yes	yes	-
	Cost of package	**$5,000 (Limited quantity)**	**$2,000 (Limited quantity)**	**Services are free**

Notes:

* The special discount is available when the guest rather than Forum organizers is paying for the accommodation

After selecting a special package, please send an email to partners@aef.kz with the name of the package, the number of persons to be accommodated, and the contact information for each. We'll email you with instructions, including paying for the package.

Week beginning	Action
December, 2011	
2 Dec	• Follow up with G20 Media • Contact Brussels media for breakfast briefing
5 Dec	• **AEF breakfast media briefing at ISC office, Brussels** • Contact FT for supplement/article on AEF • Schedule FT briefing in London
12 Dec	• Contact Brussels media for breakfast briefing • Develop content for FT special report • Issue Media briefing for global media • Project planning meeting in Astana • Contact with media ongoing • Feedback to V ASTANA Economic forum ongoing
19 Dec	• AEF breakfast media briefing, Brussels. • Event announcement: AEF delegation visit in Brussels
January 2012	
2 Jan	• Project Management meeting Astana • Prepare FT article content with AEF Organizing Committee
9 Jan	• Contact Brussels media for AEF visit in Brussels • Submit a press release: AEF delegation visit in Brussels • Discuss FT sponsorship • Brief Euractiv, BBC, Bloomberg, Reuters etc. for advertising
16 Jan	• Contact Brussels media for AEF visit in Brussels • Plan interviews for AEF visit • Contact EBS • Approach relevant individuals for interview with FT (MEPs, politicians, speakers etc.) • Prepare a media package • Prepare materials to advertise on Euractiv, BBC, Bloomberg etc.
23 Jan	• Contact Brussels media for AEF visit in Brussels • Plan interviews with AEF delegation in Brussels • Submit a press release: AEF visit in Brussels • Prepare media package, including folder, briefing notes, biographies, dossiers, visual materials etc. • Advertise on Euractiv, BBC, Bloomberg etc. • Contact Spanish media for Roundtable in Madrid • Contact Brussels media for Roundtable in Brussels • Contact UK media for Roundtable in London
30 Jan	• Follow-up with key media • Articles drafted by FT and sent for consideration • Issue invitees to media and facilitate their participation

	• Contact Spanish media for Roundtable in Madrid • Contact Brussels media for Roundtable in Brussels • Contact UK media for Roundtable in London
February	
6 Feb	• Project Management meeting Brussels • Contact Spanish media for Roundtable in Madrid (important in view of Mexico G20 and Spanish media) • Contact Brussels media for Roundtable in Brussels • Contact UK media for Roundtable in London
13 Feb	• Madrid Roundtable with Editors • Brussels Roundtable with Editors • London Roundtable with Editors (including separate meeting between FT Editors and V ASTANA leadership)
20 Feb	• Follow up on Roundtables • Begin briefing on V Astana Recommendations and assess feedback form media. This will be on-going.
27 Feb	• Final agreement between the FT and AEF regarding V ASTANA Special Report. Agree publication date and outline content.
March	
05 March	• Project Management meeting Astana • Scheduling relevant media (BBC, FT, Bloomberg, Reuters etc.) to attend V Astana
12 March	• Conference call with FT Editors, AEF Organization committee and Declan Kirrane (this will be repeated on a regular/monthly basis) • Submit a press release: AEF delegation visit in London • Media conference call with all participating Noble Laureates, including print and broadcast media (scheduled frequently in the run up to V Astana.
19 March	• Prepare a list of relevant individuals (speakers at the AEF) for interviews • Prepare a media package, including folder, briefing notes, biographies, dossiers, visual materials etc. • Contact UK media for AEF delegation visit in London
26 March	• Composition of FT Supplement article outlines • Contact UK media for AEF delegation visit in London • Submit a press release: AEF delegation visit in London • Plan interviews with AEF delegation in London • Contact relevant media (BBC, FT, Bloomberg etc.) to attend AEF in Astana • Prepare a media package, including folder, briefing notes, biographies, dossiers, visual materials etc.
April	
2 April	• Project Management meeting Brussels • AEF delegation visit in London

	• Contact relevant media (BBC, FT, Bloomberg etc.) and suggest interviews with speakers at AEF
9 April	• Follow-up • Contact media to attend AEF in Astana • Contact relevant media and suggest/plan interviews with speakers at AEF • Contact EBS to suggest publishing video after AEF
16 April	• Contact relevant media and suggest/plan interviews with speakers at AEF • Contact media for interviews with AEF Organizing Committee • Contact Brussels media for breakfast
23 April	• Publication of the FT supplement • Contact Brussels media for breakfast • Contact media for interviews with AEF Organizing Committee • Prepare a media package
30 April	• Submit a press release: V Astana Economic Forum • Contact media for interviews with AEF Organizing Committee • Prepare a media package • Contact Euractiv, BBC, Bloomberg etc. for advertising
May	
07 May	• Project Management meeting Astana • AEF breakfast at ISC office • Plan interviews with AEF participants in Astana • Prepare materials to advertise on Euractiv, BBC, Bloomberg etc.
14 May	• Plan interviews with AEF participants in Astana • Submit a press release: V Astana Economic Forum • Contact journalists that are interested in specific topics discussed at AEF – suggest stories, interviews • Advertise on Euractiv, BBC, Bloomberg etc.
21 May	• V Astana Economic Forum • May 22-24 • Forum press release • Contact journalists that are interested in specific topics discussed at AEF – suggest stories, interviews • Issue press release after AEF, focus on Conclusions • Prepare a media package on the outcomes of AEF • First announcement on VI Astana Economic Forum May 2013
28 May	• Contact journalists interested in specific topics discussed at AEF – suggest stories, interviews by way of follow up
June	

4 June	• Project Management meeting Brussels • Contact journalists that are interested in specific topics discussed at AEF – suggest stories, interviews • Follow up • Launch process focus on G20 Summit in December
11 June	• Follow up on-going
18 June	• Follow up on-going
25 June	• Intermediate report on media activities
July	
2 July	• Project Management meeting Astana • Follow up on-going
9 July	• Follow up on-going
16 July	• Follow up
23 July	• Follow up
30 July	• Planning stories with AEF Organizing Committee on different topics • Follow up
August	
6 Aug	• Project Management meeting Brussels • Follow up
13 Aug	• Follow up
20 Aug	• Follow up • Meeting with Financial Times re G20 Summit
27 Aug	• Follow up
September	
3 Sept	• Project Management meeting Astana • Contact journalists to suggest stories, interviews • Follow up
10 Sept	• Contact journalists to suggest stories, interviews • Follow up
17 Sept	• Contact Brussels media for breakfast • Follow up • Contact EBS
25 Sept	• Contact Brussels media for breakfast • Event announcement: AEF delegation visit in Brussels • Follow up • Prepare a media package • Plan EBS coverage
October	

1 Oct	• Project Management meeting Brussels • AEF breakfast at ISC office • Plan interviews with AEF delegation in Brussels • Press release after the visit
8 Oct	• Contact journalists • Prepare a media package for G20 (including in Spanish)
15 Oct	• Contact journalists • Prepare a media package for G20 (including in Spanish) • Press release: Mexico G20
22 Oct	• Plan interviews and news stories • Press release: Mexico G20 • Follow up
29 Oct	• Media Stand at the Mexico G20 Summit • Distributions of releases, video etc • Interview with V ASTANA participants
November	
5 Nov	• Project Management meeting Astana • Contact UK media for breakfast in London
12 Nov	• Contact UK media for breakfast in London
19 Nov	• Contact UK media for breakfast in London
26 Nov	• AEF Breakfast in London
December	
3 Dec	• Project Management meeting Brussels • Contact journalists to suggest stories, interviews
10 Dec	• Contact journalists to suggest stories, interviews • Plan stories on AEF topics with journalists
17 Dec	• Plan stories on AEF topics with journalists
24 Dec	• Follow up

Sections	Results	Notes
Events of the Head of State	- 2 sided meetings - 3 multilateral meetings - 1 business lunch - group photo - participation in the Grand Opening and Plenary meeting	
Events of the Prime Minister of the Republic of Kazakhstan	- 17 bilateral meetings - participation in the Grand Opening and Plenary meeting - participation in Astana Invest - participation in the Leaders Dialogue	
Organizers, co-organizers and sponsors	- 1 main coordinator - 2 main organizers - 54 co-organizers, incl. 20 foreign - more than 5 sponsors	over 50 contracts and memorandums with various suppliers

Events in the halls	- 85 events, including:
	  * 45 main events
	  * 13 subforum events
	  * 27 side events
		- 54 co-organizers, including 20 foreign
		- Live broadcast on 24.KZ
		- Live broadcast of 4 sessions with coverage of 28 events
		- Recommendations

WAC Events	- 10 events
	  * 3 panel sessions
	  * 4 round tables
	  * 2 themed dinners
	  * Leadership Dialogue
		- UNGA support, Outreach G-20, UNCTAD
		- delegates from 104 countries
		- online streaming
		- HAC Declaration
		- draft basic directions of VAP

Events in the media city area	- 12 press conferences and briefings - 2 book presentations - 1 round table - 2 days of signing memorandums and agreements - 8 TV debates - more than 300 exclusive interviews	Final press conference in the Leadership Dialogue Hall
Qualitative composition	- More than 600 speakers - More than 80 moderators	

Quantitative composition	- More than 12,500 participants from 136 countries of the world	About 3,200 foreign participants
VIP overseas	- More than 450 VIP members	Nobel laureates: 10 UN Heads: 4 Heads of State and Government (including ex-deputies): 14 Representatives of Parliament: 32 Ministers (including ex, vice): 68 Heads of banks (including deputies): 16 Ambassadors: 69 Heads and leaders of TNK: 40 Heads and managed the media: 10 Heads and leaders of international organizations: 30
Media	- More than 830 media representatives, of which 200 are foreign - Over 80 info partners: Media agency Success, CNN International, Euronews, BBC, International Herald Tribune, Rocket Media, 24 Russia, Russia Today, Khabar JSC, TC Kazakhstan, PRNewswire, Astana TC, Bilim, etc. - About 400 AEF commercials on CNN, BBC and Euronews. - Over 1,500,000 hits of AEF and G-Global banners on CNN and Euronews sites - 360 television stations, 7 news providers covering about 130 countries of the world and more than 50 hours of broadcasting - Over 12,000 photos and about 2 TB of video recording - 3,000 publications in the media, incl. 500 overseas - 100 000 common magazines, newspapers, information materials of the organizers, partners and media	- 4 Distribution of the VI AEF press release via the OVP system in 130,000 media outlets and 8 million RSS subscribers - News providers: Reuters, APTN, Cihan News Agency, Ihlas News Agency, Dogan News Agency, ABU, Fullhouse, EBU and others - International TV networks: Press TV, AZTV, Deutsche Welle, LBC-Group, Amrita TV, ARY-Digital, Asia News International, Caspio Net, Democratic Voice of Burma, Ebru TV, RTV International, Channel News Asia, RTV Slovenia and others - National TV channels: Ariana Television Network, MIS TV, ONT Belarus, Asian Television Network, BTV, SMG, Star China, Alau TV, TV 3, TV Mijas 340 TV, Tele Barn, English

	- More than 20 outputs on various channels - 30 video clips during the preparation of the AEF and events - More than 300 exclusive interviews with VIP participants (10 built-up rooms, a media corner of the Kazakhstan TC, a press corner, etc.) - More than 12 press conferences and briefings - 10 televised debates: CNN International, Euronews, EXP) -2017, AEEKU, TC Kazakhstan, Khabar and Success K - 5 final films: Success, Rocket Media, Kazakhstan TC, Korkem LLP, Prizident of Kazakhstan TV and Radio Company - creating a documentary film about "G-Global" (Khabar JSC)	Club TV, more than 40 national channels of China and others
Business and VIP meetings	- More than 100 VIP business meetings - President of the Republic of Kazakhstan: 5 meetings - Prime Minister of Kazakhstan: 17 meetings - heads of state bodies and organizations of the Republic of Kazakhstan: 82 meetings - over 20,000 meetings between delegates	- 27 business packages in the amount of 130 thousand dollars were purchased. USA
Exhibition	- More than 150 projects - 140 stands - 5 main organizers - 12 branches and directions - 12 private exhibits	Projects NATR, Kazneks, Kazagro, Kominvest, Akimatov and Parasat Holding, AEEKU, their divisions, etc.
MoU and Agreements	- 85 memorandums and agreements for 2.7 billion dollars. USA - 6 organizers - over 100 organizations and companies	
Contests	- G-Global contests in 12 nominations and TOP 50 active participants of the G-Global platform	- presentation to the winners of 12 nominations with the participation

	- about 50 thematic areas - over 120,000 participants - more than 3000 publications, 600 debates, 2000 blogs, 20,000 comments	of 4 international media experts from 4 countries
Lectures of laureates	- live lectures in 8 universities of Kazakhstan - medical lectures in 3 universities of the Republic of Kazakhstan - online lectures in 20 universities of Kazakhstan - more than 25,000 listeners	10 Nobel laureates, including 7 laureates in economics, 1 laureate in medicine, 1 laureate in physics and 1 laureate for the peace prize
Recommendations	- 110 full recommendations - More than 100 experts from 40 countries of the world, incl. from Cambridge University (UK), Yale University (USA), Club of Madrid, ITC, ILO and many other educational and research centers - More than 500 reports and messages on the G-Global platform	- Placement of recommendation in the International Herald Tribune (until June 15, 2013) - Submission of recommendation at Civic Affairs - June 12-16, 2012 - Presentation at the G20 Summit in Russia on September 5-6, 2013 - G-Global Conference in Poland - September 2013 - Submission of recommendations at UN conferences, ESCAP, UNECE, etc. (planned)
Content materials	- Issue of the Eurasian Economic Review journal - 2 issues - 1000 copies. - The release of the book: Dialectics «G-Global» under the author Nugerbekova S.N. - 1300 copies - AEEKU Magazine: G-Global megaproject - 500 copies. - Recommendations for G-20 - 400 copies. - Declaration of HAC - 500 copies. - AEF and HAC Programs - 5,000 copies. - The release of the book: N.A. Nazarbayev's Initiatives on the Formation of a New Model of the World Economy - 100 copies - Astana Journal (MFA) - 5,000 copies.	- G-Global booklet - 3000 copies. - AEF booklet - 3000 copies. - VAK booklet - 700 copies. - map - 2000 copies. - International Herald Tribune - 2 500 copies. - Explore Astana - 400 pcs. - World Economic Journal - 1,300 and etc.

	- Report of the UNCTAD Secretary General - 1,000 copies. - EFI - 135 copies. - Press kits - 500 copies.	
Astana Club Nobel Prize Laureates	- 17 laureates, including 3 new laureates with 6 AEF	- Multilateral meeting with the head of state - Business lunch with the head of state - Lectures in 28 universities of the Republic of Kazakhstan - Study in AEF and VAK - Participation in contests - Participation in TV debates - Exclusive Interviews
G-Global Board of Trustees, G-Global Global Funds	- Preparation of concepts, constituent documents, charters - Negotiations with potential donors - Business breakfast of the President of the Republic of Kazakhstan with potential members of the Board of Trustees (about 60 VIP delegates)	- Presentation at the G-Global roundtable - Adoption of the declaration - Preparation of an action plan
G-Global communication platform, AEF website, media city website, mobile platform	- 1st place in the search index on the system of Alex and Google among the economic forums (an indicator of popularity of 27 out of 100 on Alex, more than 10 million links to Google) - The AEF site in Alex's ranking among economic forums (21 thousand place among 30 million sites), G-Global site (40 thousand place) during the Forum - visitors and participants from 160 countries of the world - 120 000 users registered since the beginning of the year - about 10,000 visits per day - more than 2 300 000 visits since the beginning of the year - Over 250 news / press releases on AEF websites in various languages	- 7 sections of the portal - 5 AEEK sites - since the beginning of the year, more than 3,000 publications have been received, about 600 debates, about 2,000 blogs have been opened and over 20,000 comments have been posted. - more than 150 mailings with a base of about 1 million emails - more than 4,000 viewers of the online broadcast on the official link of the AEF

	- More than 20,000 users of the mobile platform - More than 20,000 comments on the G-Global platform - Over 500 posts on Twitter - More than 30,000 friends on social pages on Facebook, Twitter, Linked, etc. - More than 500 banners and links on various sites - More than 500 videos on YouTube	
Support Group and Logistics	- 11 hotel partners, 183 rooms with a discount - 115 tickets redeemed - 53 VIP cars, 63 business class units, 45 buses and 45 minivans - meals for 10,000 people 110 volunteers - 96 translators - 70 photo and video operators - 250 accompanying, incl. 85 VIP accompanying	- 3 food suppliers - 1 transport supplier - 1 provider for sites and registrations - 10 accommodation providers - 1 synchronous equipment supplier - 3 vendors for the design of rooms - 2 vendors for TCP - 1 supplier for PR, photo and video - 6 suppliers of foreign lighting - 3 ICT infrastructure providers - key co-organizers and government agencies
Virtual VI AEF and WAC (April 19 - May 19)	- 40 co-organizers participated, - 68 online conferences held, - 693 reports and 79 recommendations received at the AEF, 37 reports at the Higher Attestation Commission	
Perspectives and ideas from AEF	- Creating a Sustainable Development Fund; - The creation of the TV channel G-Global; - Creation of the Kazakh version of the TV channel Euronews; - Opening of the regional office of Euronews;	- More than 3,000 foreign tourists and potential distributors of information about Kazakhstan - More than 6,000 domestic tourists in Kazakhstan

	- Opening of the UN regional hub in Almaty; - Formation of the G-Global expert commission with the support of the UN.	

This document is translated in Google from Russian.

V ASTANA ECONOMIC FORUM

May 22-24, 2012

OPENING CEREMONY AND PLENARY SESSION

FINANCIAL CAPITAL AND WORLD ECONOMY	INDUSTRIAL AND INNOVATIVE DEVELOPMENT	RESOURCE AND FOOD SECURITY
The crisis in the global financial structural system	Investment forum Astana Invest 2012	Kazakhstan's energy and ecological initiatives
Opportunities and problems of economic integration	Business innovation – the way to a competitive economy	The Customs Union's common agricultural hub
Seminar on improving competitiveness	Businesswomen's forum	Coming trends in managing fossil-energy resources
Macroeconomic development and forecasting	II Eurasian Business Congress	Strategic planning for the transition to a sustainable economy
Public-private partnership investments in tourism – a key to sustainable development of the industry in Kazakhstan	Challenges to development of the medical and pharmaceutical industries	
Asian business leadership: Factors in its success	Effective entrepreneurship/ efficient economy	
Globalization's influence on socio-economic development and regional integration: Do we have the correct figures?	Practical applications of public-private partnerships in Kazakhstan's economy	
Stock markets: the world of IPOs	Intellectual property's role in economic growth	
Economic policy based on Parametrical Regulation Theory	Eurasian ICT forum "Connect Kazakhstan"	
	Perspectives on developing Kazakhstan's transportation infrastructure	
	Modernizing the civil service for a changing world	
	Generating good jobs in the	

	context of today's global employment trends	

BRIEFING: "DIALOGUE OF LEADERS: CHANGING GLOBAL FINANCIAL POLICY"

MEETING OF FINANCE MINISTERS OF CIS STATES

MEETING OF EDUCATIONAL MINISTERS OF MEMBERS OF THE ORGANIZATION OF ISLAMIC COOPERATION ORGANIZATION

EURASIAN ECONOMIC YOUTH FORUM

FREE ZONE: BUSINESS CULTURE

Exhibition of investment projects	Benefit concert	Regional exhibition "Industrial and Innovative Potential of Kazakhstan"
ICT exhibition	Kazakhstan's Shapagat innovation awards	

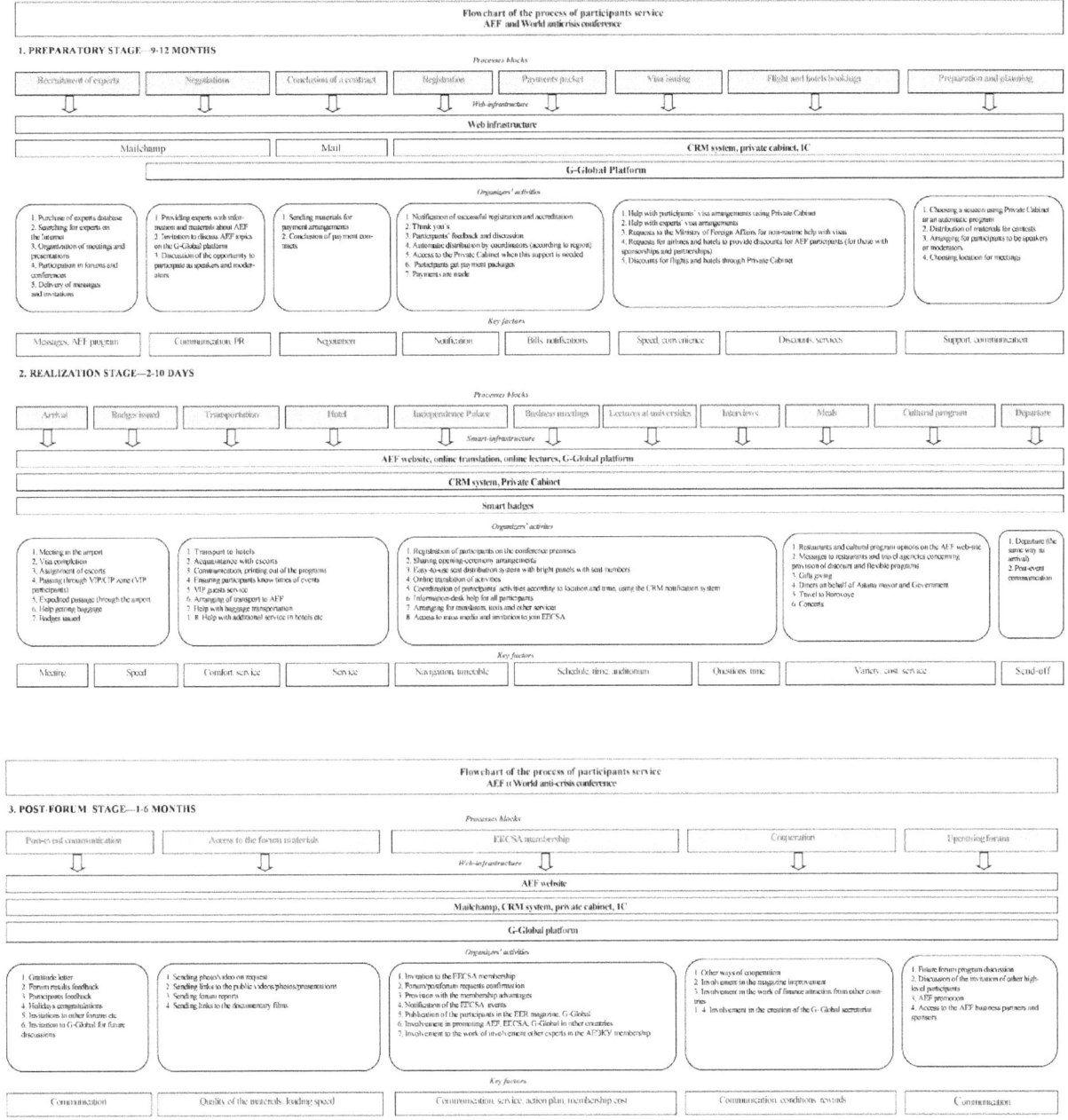

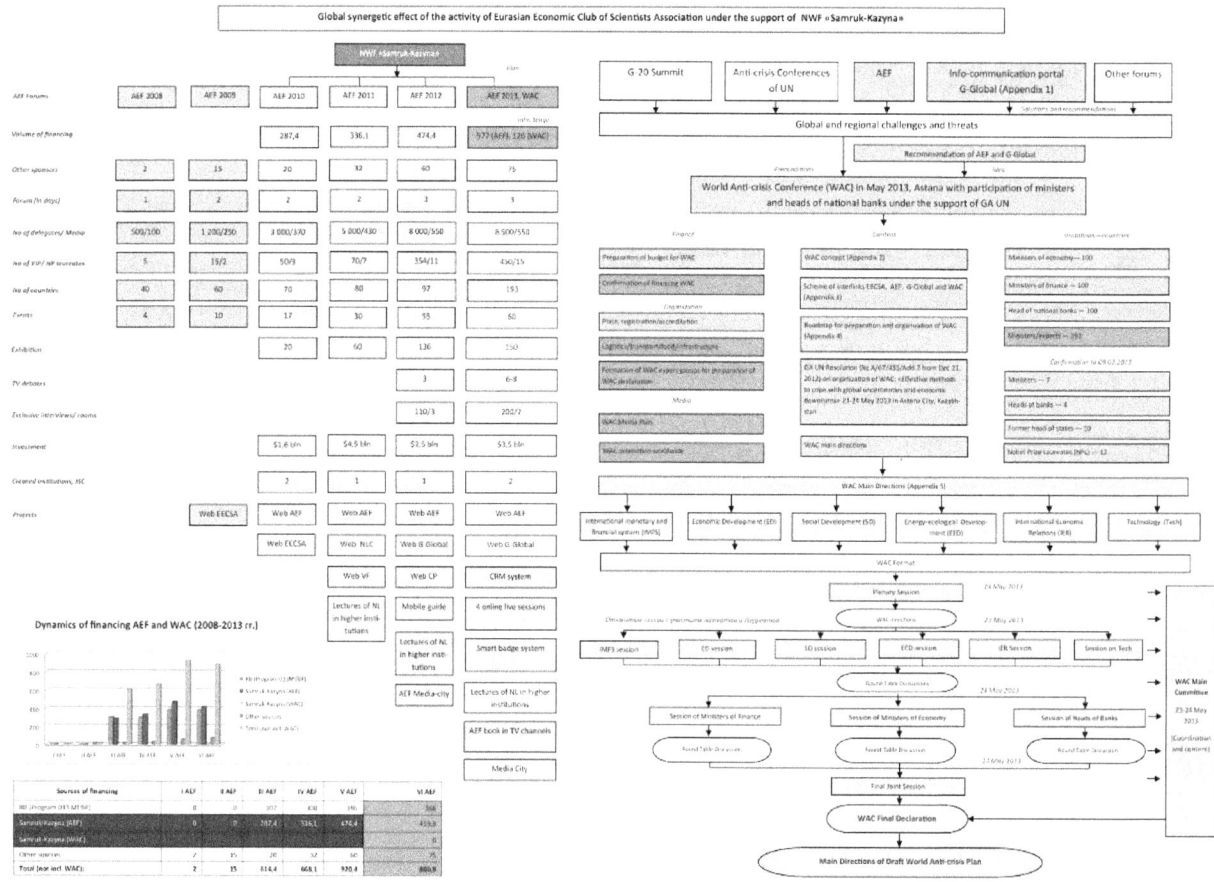

ПРЕЗИДИУМ/Presidium

1 сектор 1 sector	Сектор 2 2 sector	Сектор 3 3 sector	Сектор 4 4 sector	Сектор 5 5 sector	Сектор 6 6 sector	Сектор 7 7 sector

СХЕМА РАССАДКИ
на IV Астанинском экономическом форуме

The seating arrangement of the
IV Astana Economic Forun

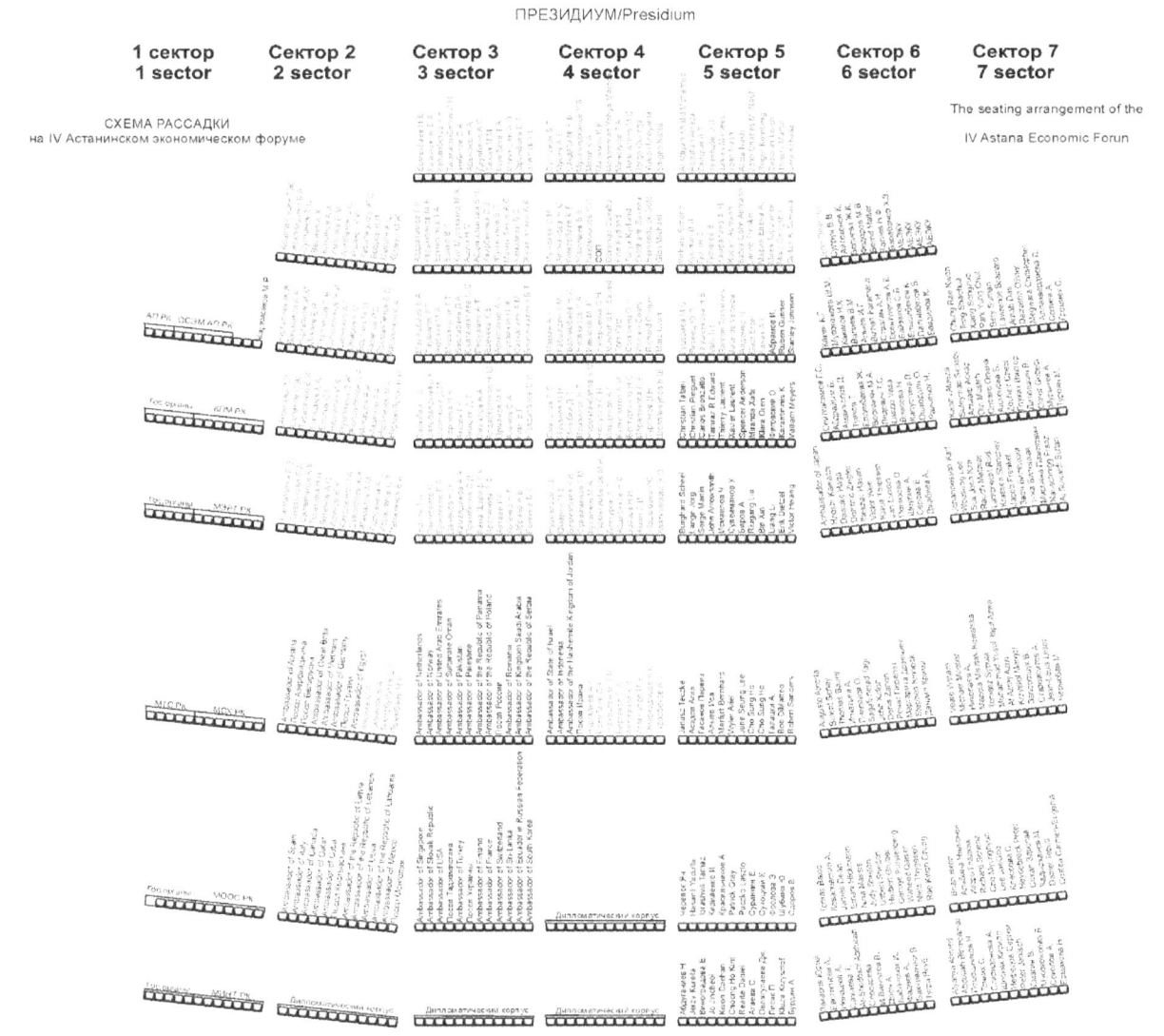

Общий свод по подготовке АЭФ   27.03.2019

Дата: 24 марта 2012	Устное или письменное подтверждение						Электронная регистрация							Участ. потенц. (5000)	Всего											
	Приглашения			Подтверждения			Регистрация			Аккредитация					Страны (80)	ВИП (Intl) (200)	ВИП (Каз) (150)	Спикер (366)	Модер. (52)	ЛНП (10)	Главы стран (10)+ех	ПМ (10)+ех	Министры (20)+ех	Рук.банков (20)	Рук.ТНК (20)	Рук.СМИ (10)
	КАЗ	INTL	Отказ	ВСЕГО прит.	КАЗ (3500)	INTL (1500)	ВСЕГО (5000)	Каз. 3500	INTL 1500	не указ.	ВСЕГО	Каз.	INTL	ВСЕГО													
Количество	2249	7288	243	9537	0	329	329	1086	254	50	1390	142	212	354	1719	116	293		295	43	9	8	9	21	15	36	5
Выполняемость (%)			3%			22%	7%							34%					81%	83%	75%	80%	90%				50%

Наименование	По странам приглаш.				Отправитель писем			Аудитория	Сервисы и Поддержка					Участники		Резюме (3 из.) (1140)	Доклады спикеров ()	Сценарий модератора ()	Фото ()	Спикер (366)	Модер. (52)	Участие					
	КАЗ	INTL	Отказ	ВСЕГО	Соорган. +другие	ГИС Акорда	АЕЭКУ		Виза ()	Авиа ()	Отель ()	Авто ()	Перевод ()	Выбор	ВИП							ГТ, ПМ	ЛНП	Министры	Рук.банк	ТНК	СМИ
Connect Kazakhstan	25	27		27				700	2											19из32							
Форум Молодежи	200	15	10	215	15			300	23							24				38	7из8					
2 ЕАДК	61	123		184	120			150	5											4из6	1					
Интеллектуальная собств.	143	27		170				100	3							26				20	1					
ГЧП в экономике Каз.	30	86		136				280								36				11	1					
Транспортная инфр-ра		85	8		64			100	1											8из11	1					
Торж. открытие		5000	225	5000		3205	637	3000	36											8	1					
Совещание министров СНГ		66		66				66									нет			7	1					
ГЭЭФ- 1,2,3	212	147		359	359			300	15							45				19из26	5					
Иннов. Конгресс (1-4)	100	50			4			300	4											5из7	1					
ГЧП в туризм		251		251				280	3											11из12						
Эра иск. источников энерг.	20	90						150	3											5из7	1					
Эконом. Интеграция	78	44			14			150	4											8из10	1					
Астана Инвест	393	432		825	751			500												5из10	2из4					
МФА	200	250		450		240		300	14							28				22из25	5					
Эффект. Предпринимат.	257	61		318	175			280	4							24				8	1					
Единый сельхоз хаб	10	150		160	160			100	3											7из8	1					
Конкурентоспособность	105	33						150												5из6	1					
Мир IPO	141	26		167				150	2											5из6	1					
Медицина и фармацевтика	60	90		150	23			150	10											7	1					
Модернизация Гос. службы		100		100				100												10из12	2					
Азиатское лидерство	84	55						150	1											3из5	1					
Влияние глоб. Прав. Циф.	130	20						280	9							27				8из10	2					
Эконом. Политика									4											10из11						
Достойный труд		10						150												3из5	1					
Модели стран. Партнеров.		50						100	1											4из7	1					
Конкурс Шапагат								300												н/б	2					
Лекции лауреатов				24 вуз				4800												12	н/б					
Диалог лидеров				0				1000	7						133	28				20						
ВСЕГО	2249	7288	243	9537	1712	3445	637	14386	154							315				295из366	43из52					
Выполняемость																36%				81%	83%					
Оплачиваемые																										

Выставка индустриально-инновационных проектов	Необход. Пл. (м2)	Выделено (м2)	Наличие концепции	Место во Дворце	Количество предоставленных проектов	Количество отобранных проектов	Утвер.	Утверждение дизайна	Бюджет	Заключение соглашений	Количество стендов
ИИФ	200	200	-	3 этаж	30			-			
Комин вест/Коглен и Акимату											
РК	250	250	-	2 этаж	116			-	на рассм		
Казагро	50	50	-	1 этаж	10			-			
Акимат Астаны	200	200	-	1 этаж	30			-			
Холдинг Зерде	Media Center		-	Media Center							
Всего	700	700			186						
Выставка частных компаний											
Международный торговый центр	7	7		1 этаж							
Астана Солар	15	15		2 этаж							
Всего	22	22									

Наименование	Сайты (на 24 марта)			
	АЭФ/GG	АЕЭКУ	ЛНП	Йод
Рейтинг алекса (мировой) 3 мес	49 838	946 283	4 708 034	1 107 102
Рейтинг (КАЗ)	150	4624		
Ссылки	180	37	18	20
Посещений в день	4425			

Наименование	Давос	ПМЭФ	ВИЭФ	Economist Conferences
Рейтинг алекса	28 170	865 404	1 629 799	627 600
Рейтинг (в стране)	50 491	60 955	11 340	74 999
Ссылки	10 630	366	43	374
Посещений в день				

AGENDA
V ASTANA ECONOMIC FORUM

May 22-24, 2012, Astana

The latest program is available at www.aef.kz

	MAY 21 **PRE-FORUM DAY**
10:00-18:00 «Beijing Palace Soluxe Hotel Astana», "Soluxe" Hall (27, Syganak Str.)	**"CONNECT KAZAKHSTAN"** **EURASIAN ICT FORUM**
	Organizers: *Ministry of Transport and Communications of the Republic of Kazakhstan, JSC "Zerde" National ICT Holding, Communicative company "United Agencies C I"*
	Questions for discussion: *- Technology innovations creating sustainability and economic growth.* *- ICT standard regulations.* *- E-government: modern vision of Kazakhstan.* *- ICT investments: synthesis of financial tools and innovations.*
	OPENING
10:00-10:15	Welcome Speech: **Askar Zhumagaliyev,** Minister of Transport and Communications of the Republic of Kazakhstan
Theme of the day	**VALUE CREATED BY ICT SECTOR**
10:15-11:30	**SESSION:** **INNOVATIONS AND TECHNOLOGIES CREATING SUSTAINABILITY AND ECONOMIC GROWTH**
	Speakers:
	Nurlan Izmailov, Chairman of JSC "Zerde" National ICT Holding
	Leonid Altuhov, Vice-President, Director of Regional Development, IBM in Russia and CIS
	Stephen Ibaraki, Investor, writer, IT professional
	Victor Griban, Chief Operating Officer at 2DayTelecom, Kazakhstan
12:00-13:00	**SESSION:** **E-GOVERNMENT: MODERN VISION OF KAZAKHSTAN**
	Speakers:

	Arvo Ott, E-Governance Academy Board Member, Estonia
	Ruslan Yensebayev, Chairman of the Board, "National Information Technologies" JSC
13:00-14:00	**SESSION:** **ICT INVESTMENTS: SYNTHESIS OF FINANCIAL TOOLS AND INNOVATIONS**
	Speakers:
	Petri Karinen, Head of the International Affairs Business Oulu, Finland
	Ben de Beer, HP, Netherlands
16:00-17:30	**SESSION:** **ICT INNOVATIONS ARE CHANGING CONSUMER HABITS**
	Speakers:
	Mark Mueller-Eberstein, Author of "Agility: Competing and Winning in the Tech Savvy Marketplace"
	Petko Draganov, Deputy Secretary-General of UNCTAD
	Natalia Novikova, LG Electronics Almaty Kazakhstan
	Sergey Sergeyev, HP, Ukraine

	MAY 22
09:30-18:00 «Beijing Palace Soluxe Hotel Astana», "Soluxe" Hall (27, Syganak Str.)	**EURASIAN ICT FORUM "CONNECT KAZAKHSTAN"**
Theme of the day	**REMARKABLE INNOVATIONS IN ICT SECTOR**
	Organizers: *Ministry of Transport and Communications of the Republic of Kazakhstan, JSC "Zerde" National ICT Holding, Communicative Company "United Agencies CA"*
	Questions for discussion: *- ICT innovations are changing business habits.* *- ICT future vision: plans, solutions and prospects.*
9:30-11:00	**SESSION:** **ICT INNOVATIONS ARE CHANGING BUSINESS HABITS**
	Speakers:
	Liudvikas Andriulis, Chief Marketing Specialist of "Effortel"
	Jari Tammisto, CEO and President of Mobile Monday Global
	Niklas Henricson, Head of Communications of TeliaSonera Business Services division, Sweden
	Sergey Nazarenko, Manager of Program Management Section, Kcell, Kazakhstan
	Eberhard Bluemel, Fraunhofer Institute for Factory Operation and Automation, Germany

11:30-12:15	SESSION: ICT FUTURE: PLANS, SOLUTIONS AND PROSPECTS
	Speaker:
	Ian Pearson, Futurologist and Former Leading IT Advisor of British Telecom

14:00-18:00	CONNECT DIGITAL
14:00-14:05	OPENING
14:05-15:30	KEYNOTE: THE INTERNET AS A SOCIAL PHENOMENON
	Speakers:
	Mads Holmen, Planning Director, Go Viral
14:50-15:30	KNOWLEDGE, CREATIVITY, FUTURE AND... COSMOS!
	Speaker:
	Vladas Lashas, Businessman, Founder of organization "Carbon War Room", Republic of Lithuania
15.30-16.30	STARTUP SESSION
	Speakers:
	Bolat Bashayev, Founder and CEO of ARTA, (Kazakhstan)
	Startup presentations
16:00-16:45	THE NEW GENERATION OF COMMUNICATION
	Speakers:
	Sture Udd, Founder and CEO "Up Code", Finland
17:30-18:00	PERSPECTIVES FOR SOCIAL MEDIA COMMUNICATION IN KAZAKHSTAN
	Speaker:
	Tomas Nemura, Chief Executive Officer at digital agency "The Chocolate", Republic of Lithuania
18:00-18:30	ONLINE + OFFLINE = SUCCESS. ONLINE SHOP BFF.KZ
	Улан Каражигитов, Founder, E-Shop BFF.Kz, Kazakhstan
	Рустем Карымов, Founder, E-Shop BFF.Kz, Kazakhstan

10:00-18:30 L.N. Gumilyov ENU's Conference Hall (5, Munaitpasova str.)	WORLD ECONOMIC YOUTH FORUM
	THE PLACE AND ROLE OF YOUTH IN ECONOMIC MODERNIZATION
	Organizers:

	L.N. Gumilyov Eurasian National University, Ural State Economic University, Kazakh University of Economics, Finance and International Trade, Youth Directorate of Eurasian Economic Club of Scientists *With support of:* *Ministry of Education and Science of the Republic of Kazakhstan*
10:00-12:30	**PLENARY SESSION**
	Moderator: **Yerlan Sydykov**, Rector of the L.N. Gumilyov Eurasian National University, Doctor of Historical Sciences, Professor, Academician of International Academy of Science of Pedagogical Education
	Welcome Speech: **Robert Aumann**, Nobel Prize winner in Economics 2005, "for his work on conflict and cooperation through game-theory analysis", Professor of Hebrew University of Jerusalem, Israel
	Mikhail Fedorov, Chairman of the EEFM Organizing Committee, Deputy Chairman of the Coordination Council of the "Eurasian Economic Club of Scientists" Association, President ANO "Great Eurasian university complex", Rector of the Ural State Economic University, an official Ambassador of EXPO-2020 Application, Doctor of Economic Sciences, Professor, Russian Federation
	Sarsengali Abdymanapov, The Rector of the Kazakh University of Economy, Finance and International Trade, International Academy of Higher Education, Doctor of Pedagogical Sciences, Professor
	Eric Maskin, Nobel Prize winner in Economics 2007, for having laid the foundations of mechanism design theory, Professor of Harvard University, USA
	Danyiar Medetov, 1st year student, L.N. Gumilyov Eurasian National University, owner of the "Altyn Belgy" award
	Speakers: **Bernd Hallier**, Head of the International Trade Institute, President of European Trade Association, Germany
	Gabriel Kochofa Aniset, Ambassador Extraordinary and Plenipotentiary of Republic Benin in Russian Federation, President of the Association of Foreign Students in Russia
	Patricio Chaves Savala, Special and Authorized Ambassador of Ecuador Republic in Russian Federation
	Ivan Vozmilov, Head of the Youth Department of Eurasian Economic Youth Forum
13:30-15:30	**PRESENTATION SESSION RUSSIA-KAZAKHSTAN**
	A STUDENT TODAY – AN EXPONENT TOMORROW **THE ROLE OF EXPO EXHIBITION IN THE DEVELOPMENT OF REGIONAL ECONOMICS**
	Organizer: *Ural State Economic University*
	Questions for discussion:

	- The role of EXPO exhibition for regional and national economics of countries: counties participants experience and prospects for Russia and Kazakhstan. *- EXPO exhibition as a means of increasing investment attractiveness of regions and business development.* *- EXPO's role in territories marketing and cities branding.* *- EXPO as a platform of the ethno-cultural communication for tolerance formation in terms of globalization.* *- Attraction of the youth potential for EXPO promotion in Yekaterinburg and Astana.*
	Presentations of assembly University team of Kazakhstan and winner team of EEFY contests: *- The role of EXPO-2017 exhibition in the economic development of the Republic of Kazakhstan.* *- The role of EXPO-2020 exhibition in development of Russian Federation economics.*
	Moderator: **Elena Ovsyannikova,** Director of Congress "EXPO-2020" the third Eurasian Economic Youth Forum, Director of finance and law department of State Economic University.
	Participants: Kazakhstan Universities joint team, Winners of EEFY contests.
	Experts:
	Mikhail Fedorov, Chairman of the EEFM Organizing Committee, Deputy Chairman of the Coordination Council of the "Eurasian Economic Club of Scientists" Association, President ANO "Great Eurasian university complex", Rector of the Ural State Economic University, Official Ambassador of EXPO-2020 Application, Doctor of Economic Sciences, Professor, Russian Federation
	Aidar Kazybayev, Chairman of the Trade Committee of Ministry of Economic Development and Trade of the Republic of Kazakhstan
	Miguel de la Cruz Salcedo, Press attaché of Ecuador Republic Embassy in Russia, President of Latin American sector AIS, Ecuador
	Gabriel Kochofa Aniset, Ambassador Extraordinary and Plenipotentiary of Republic Benin in Russian Federation, President of the Association of Foreign Students in Russia
	Martin Valtiner, Accredited Architectural Engineer, Owner of Architectural Bureau of Civil Engineering "Valtiner and Partners", Austria
	Nasirzhon Abduganiyev, Vice Chancellor of CIS University, Russian Federation
	Speakers:
	Aidar Kazybayev, Chairman of the Trade Committee, Ministry of Economic Development and Trade, Republic of Kazakhstan
	Experts and members recommendations on forming a positive outlook among people of countries and regions on EXPO exhibition

	Presentation of Kazakhstan Universities team **"What does our youth do for winning EXPO 2017 in Astana"**
	Questions and answers upon theme agenda
	Presentation of the EEFY competition winners **The role of EEFY in promotion of EXPO 2020 claim in Yekaterinburg**
	Questions and answers upon presentation
	Speakers:
	Mikhail Fedorov, Chairman of the EEFY Organizing Committee, Deputy Chairman of the Coordination Council of the "Eurasian Economic Club of Scientists" Association, President ANO "Great Eurasian university complex", Rector of the Ural State Economic University, Official Ambassador of EXPO-2020 Application, Doctor of Economic Sciences, Professor, Russian Federation
	Show case "Flash-mob- as an effective form of the application promotion for the right of EXPO exhibition conduction" (Russia-Kazakhstan: Joint flash-mob of participants and experts)
13:30-15:30	**PANEL DISCUSSION 2** **«YOUTH RECOMMENDATIONS FOR G-20 COUNTRIES»**
	Organizer: *L.N. Gumilyov Eurasian National University*
	Questions for discussion: *- World currency system in the world financial crisis conditions. The analysis of existing global calls and problems in functioning of world currency system. Recommendations about world financial system reforming and expected results of it.* *- Right protection of results of intellectual activity in the World. Development and protection of intellectual property rights. Intellectual property in innovative economy: patents and know-how. Intellectual property in an education sphere and creativity.* *- Preservation and an effective utilization of monuments of history and culture for development of republican and international tourism, propaganda of rich historical and cultural heritage of Kazakhstan at an international level.*
	Moderator: **Balsheker Alibekova,** Dean of the Faculty of Economics, L.N. Gumilyov Eurasian National University
	Speakers:
	Choong Y. Lee, Professor of Pittsburg State University, USA
	Janusz Taszke, Professor of Economic University in Krakov, Poland
	Jay Natan, Professor of St. Johns University, NY,USA
	Philipp Missfelder, Member of the German Bundestag, elected Foreign Policy Spokesman of the CDU / CSU parliamentary group, Federal President of the Junge Union
	RECOMMENDATIONS OF STUDENTS TEAMS WITHIN THE LIMITS OF KEY THEMES
	Participants:

	Students commands of: - Ural State Economic University - L.N. Gumilyov Eurasian National University - Kazakh University of Economics, Finance and International Trade
	Discussion of offers, opinion of experts and judges, summarizing Resolution acceptance
	CONTEST **INNOVATION PROJECTS OF PROFESSOR W.SCHARFF**
	Moderator: **Wolfram Scharff,** Professor of Technical University, Chemnitz, Germany
	Awarding of Winners
13:30-15:30	**PANEL DISCUSSION 3** **PROSPECTS OF YOUNG SCIENTISTS IN CONTEMPORARY CONDITIONS**
	Organizer: *Kazakh University of Economics, Finance and International Trade*
	Questions for discussion: *- Discussion of current achievements, opportunities and problems of young scientists in the CIS countries, the possible scenarios and prospects of development of international and interregional cooperation in spheres of science and education.* *- Acquaintance with examples of the most successful practices in this direction and exchange of experience in solution of problems.* *- VIewing the opportunities to enhance academic mobility and the development of cooperation between young scientists of the CIS.* *- Experience of research training within the Bologna system in the Republic of Kazakhstan.*
	Moderator: **Amina Musina,** Vice-Rector for Science and International Relations of the Kazakh University of Economy, Finance and International Trade, Doctor of Economic Sciences, Professor
	Speakers: **Ayan Zhumashev,** Deputy Chairman of the "One junior organization "Zhas Ulan", 4th year student majoring in "Accounting and Auditing"
	Aliya Shakharova, Chairman of the Board of Young Scientists of the Kazakh University of Economy, Finance and International Trade, PhD in Economics, Assistant Professor
	Baurzhan Sarmurzin, Master of Economics, Member of the Young Scientists of the Kazakh University of Economics, Finance and International Trade
	Irina Neganova, Chairman of the Board of Young Scientists of the Ural State Economic University, Russian Federation
	John E. Endicott, President of Woosong University and Vice-Chancellor of SolBridge International School of Business Daejeon, Republic of South Korea
	Rahman Alshanov, Rector of "Turan" University, President of the Association of Universities of the Republic of Kazakhstan, Doctor of Economic Sciences, Professor, Academician of the Engineering Academy

	Nodir Zhumayev, Rector of the Tashkent State Economic University, Doctor of Economic Sciences, Professor, Republic of Uzbekistan
	Olena Slezko Institute of World Economy and International Relations (IWEIR) NAS Ukraine (Kiev), Top Research Adviser of Department International Finance Relations
	Bernd Hallier, Director of the International Institute of Retail, Executive of the European Retail Academy, Germany
	PARTICIPANTS OF DISCUSSION
	Nadezhda Parusimova, Head of the Department of Banking and Insurance of the Orenburg State University, Doctor of Economic Sciences, Russian Federation
	Iskandar Yuldashev, Regional Manager, Solbridge International School of Business, Woosong University Daejeon, Republic of South Korea
	Vladimir Nifadyev, Doctor of Economic Science, Professor, Rector of the Kyrgyz-Russian Slavic University after B.N. Yeltsin
	Saydilla Gulyamov, Chairman of the Board of Young Scientists of the Academy of Sciences of Uzbekistan, Doctor of Law, Professor, Republic of Uzbekistan
	Marat Safiullin, Pro-rector for Economic and Strategic Development of Kazan Federal University, Doctor of Economic Sciences, Academician of the Academy of Science of the Republic of Tatarstan
16:00-18:00	**«GENERATIONS SOLIDARITY – THE BRIDGE TO THE FUTURE» FINAL SESSION OF APPLICANTS FOR THE YOUTH PRIZE**
	Moderator: **Mikhail Fedorov,** Chairman of the EEFY Organizing Committee, Deputy Chairman of the Coordination Council of the "Eurasian Economic Club of Scientists" Association, President ANO "Great Eurasian university complex", Rector of the Ural State Economic University, Official Ambassador of EXPO-2020 Application, Doctor of Economic Sciences, Professor, Russian Federation
	Finalists competition for the Youth Prize
	Participants of Discussion:
	Finn Kydland, Nobel Prize winner in Economics 2004 "for contributions to dynamic macroeconomics: the time consistency of economic policy and the driving forces behind business cycles", Professor of the University of Santa Barbara, California, USA
	Mark Uzan, Executive Director Reinventing Bretton Woods Committee
	Nick Bostrom, Philosopher, Professor of Oxford University, Director of Future Mankind University at Oxford University
	Jamais Cascio, Research Fellow, Institute for the Future; Senior Fellow, Institute for Ethics and Emerging Technologies. Selected by "Foreign Policy" magazine as one of their Top 100 Global Thinkers (2009)
	Hans Rosling, Professor of International Health at Karolinska Institute, Founder of "Gapminder" Fund
	Hanon Barabaner, Rector of Economic and Administration Institute, Doctors of Economic Sciences, Professor, Estonia

	Laszlo Vasas, Dean of the Saint Istvan, Hungary
	Nuriddin Kayumov, Director of the Economic Research Institute of the Ministry of Economic Development and Trade of the Republic of Tajikistan, Doctor of Economic Sciences, Professor
	Edward Sandoyan, Pro-rector on development of University education at Russian-Armenian (Slavic) University, Doctor of Economic Sciences, Professor
	Ian Campbell, Professor of Prague Economic University, Czech Republic
	Italo Trevisan, Professor of Trento University, Italy
	Elena Ermolaeva, Associate Professor of the Riga High School of Economy and Culture, Principal investigator of the Riga Academy of Pedagogy and Educational Administration, Republic of Latvia
	Marin Marinov, Assistant Professor of Newcastle University, Great Britain
19:00-22:00	**FRIENDSHIP BALL, DEVOTED TO AWARDING OF "EURASIAN STARS" AND ANNOUNCING OF THE YOUTH PRIZE LAUREATE**

10:00-13:00 Press Center Hall, Palace of Independence, Ground Floor (5, Tauelsizdik str.)	**PANEL SESSION** **MACROECONOMIC POLICY, INSTRUMENTS OF MACROECONOMIC FORECASTING AND REGULATION**
	Organizers: *The Kazakh National Technical University after K.Satpayev, Institute of Information Science and Control of the Ministry of Education and Science of the Republic of Kazakhstan* *Support: USAID Macroeconomic Project*
	Questions for discussion: *- What expectations does the world economy have in 2012-2013: turbulence or "ideal storm"?* *- Macroeconomic policy of countries with developing markets: growth limits and transition to new models of growth.* *- Analysis of economies of developing countries: responses to the challenges of the changing world.* *- Kazakhstan's experience in building operational monitoring and short-term forecast of the economy of Kazakhstan in the period of instability of the world economy.* *- Elements of the theory of parametrical regulation of national economy.* *- Macroeconomic analysis, parametrical regulation and development of recommendations in the sphere of economic growth on the basis of the number of computable general equilibrium models and dynamical stochastic general equilibrium models.* *- Parametrical regulation of characteristics of market cycles and influence of shocks on national economy evolution based on the number of macroeconomic models.*

		- Macroeconomic analysis and parametrical regulation of stabilizing policy based on the static model of small open economy. *- Information decision support system based on parametrical regulation theory.*
10:00-11:15	**Moderator:**	
	Rakhman Alshanov, Rector of "Turan" University, President for the Association of Universities of the Republic of Kazakhstan, Doctor of Economic Sciences, Professor, Academician of the Engineering Academy	
	Speakers:	
	Finn Kydland, Nobel Prize winner in Economics 2004 "for contributions to dynamic macroeconomics: the time consistency of economic policy and the driving forces behind business cycles", Professor of the University of Santa Barbara, California, USA	
	Edward Prescott, Nobel Memorial Prize winner in Economics 2004, "for contributions to dynamic macroeconomics: the time consistency of economic policy and the driving forces behind business cycles", Professor at Arizona State University, USA	
	Sara Alpysbayeva, Head of the Center of Macroeconomic Analysis and Strategic Research at "Economic Research Institute" JSC, Doctor of Economic Sciences, Professor	
	Sailau Baizakov, Scientific Supervisor, "Economic Research Institute" JSC, Doctor of Economic Sciences, Professor	
	Abdykappar Ashimov, Scientific Supervisor of the State Scientific and Technical Program, Doctor of Technical Sciences, Professor, Member of the National Academy of Sciences of the Republic of Kazakhstan	
	Yuriy Borovskiy, Deputy Chairman of Scientific State Program, Associate Professor	
11:40-13:00	**Moderator:**	
	Abdykappar Ashimov, Scientific Supervisor of the State Scientific and Technical Program, Doctor of Technical Sciences, Professor, Member of the National Academy of Sciences of the Republic of Kazakhstan	
	Speakers:	
	Rakhman Alshanov, Rector of "Turan" University, President for the Association of Universities of the Republic of Kazakhstan, Doctor of Economic Sciences, Professor, Academician of the Engineering Academy	
	Dmitry Novikov, Deputy Head of the Management Research Institute of the Russian Science Academy, Corresponding Member of the RSA, Doctor of Technical Sciences, Professor	
	Nikolay Borovsky, Research Associate of the State Scientific and Stechnical Program	
	Mukhit Onalbekov, Scientific Officer of the State Scientific and Technical Program	
	Dauren Aidarkhanov, Scientific Officer of the State Scientific and Technical Program	
	Nurlan Sailaubekov, Head of the Department of Economy and Logistics at the International Academy of Business, Doctor of Economic Sciences, Associate Professor	

	Igor Janishevskiy, Scientific Officer of the State Scientific and Technical Program, Candidate of Physical-Mathematical Sciences
	Igor Pospelov, Head of Economic systems' mathematical modeling department at the RSA Computing center after A.A. Dorodnitsin, Corresponding Member of the RSA
	Galimkair Mutanov, Rector of Al-Farabi Kazakh National University, Doctor of Technical Sciences, Professor
	Maksat Kalimoldayev, Director of the Information Science and Management Institute of the Ministry of Education of the Republic of Kazakhstan, Doctor in Technical Science, Professor
	Alida Ashimbayeva, "Turan" University, Professor, Doctor of Economic Sciences
	Ergali Dosmagambet, Director, Department for Research Administration of Nazarbayev University, PhD
	Mars Gabbasov, Deputy General Director for science of CSS "Factor" ltd, Candidate of physical-mathematical sciences, Associate professor

10:00-13:00 Palace of Independence, Oval hall, Ground Floor	**ROUND TABLE** **MODEL OF STRATEGIC PLANNING FOR THE TRANSITION TO A SUSTAINABLE ECONOMY**
	Organizers: *Higher Party School of PDP "Nur Otan", Global Green Growth Institute, Economic Research Institute JSC, UNDP, NESDCA*
	Questions for discussion: *- Approaches to develop a new model of strategic planning for the transition to a sustainable economy.* *- Search for answers to global environmental, economic and social challenges of our time.* *- Development and implementation of innovative methods of strategic planning and management in partnership with business and the demonstration area of "green solutions".* *- Development of Kazakhstan National Green Growth Plan (KNGGP), the new approach to strategic planning.* *- Development of recommendations and priorities for cooperation in the framework of new approaches to the system of strategic planning at the global and regional levels.*
	Moderator:
	Bakhyt Yessekina, Director of the Higher Party School of PDP "Nur Otan", Doctor of Economic Sciences, Professor
	Welcome Speech:
	Kairat Kelimbetov, Deputy Prime Minister of the Republic of Kazakhstan
	Lord Waverley, Chair of Central Asia Parliamentary Group, UK Parliament
	Myung-Kyoon Lee, Director, Country Program & Knowledge Integration Unit GGGI, Republic of South Korea
	Speakers:

	Joan Clos, Executive Director of United Nations Human Settlements Programme (UN-HABITAT)
	Ruslan Grinberg, Director of Economics Institute , Russian Academy of Sciences, Russian Federation
	Maksat Mukhanov, President of the "Institute for Economic Research" JSC, Republic of Kazakhstan
	Joo Sueb Lee, Senior Program Manager Global Green Growth Institute, Republic of Korea
	Gleb Fetisov, Head of Council on Investigation of Productive Forces (SOPS), Member of Public Chamber under the President of the Russian Federation, Doctor of Economic Sciences, Professor
	Stephen Tull, UN Resident Coordinator, UNDP Representative in Kazakhstan, Doctor of Political Sciences
	Hanon Barabaner, Rector of Institute of Economy «ECOMEN», Deputy Chairman of Coordination Council "Eurasian Economic Club of Scientists" Association, Doctor of Economic Sciences, Professor, Estonia

14:30-18:00 Palace of Independence, Ceremonial Hall, Ground Floor	**I STATE – BUSINESS PARTNERSHIP CONGRESS "ATTRACTING PRIVATE INVESTMENT FOR THE DEVELOPMENT OF PUBLIC SERVICES IN KAZAKHSTAN"**
	Organizers: *Ministry of Economic Development and Trade of the Republic of Kazakhstan, JSC "Kazakhstan Public-Private Partnership Center"*
	Questions for discussion: *- Methods of creating conditions for implementation of projects in various sectors of the economy.* *- Methods of attracting private investment in infrastructure development.* *- Improving the legal framework of PPP.* *- Enhancement of the PPP institutional system.* *- Enhancement of the effectiveness of state support measures for PPP projects.* *- International best practice in financing PPP projects.*
14:30-15:15	**PLENARY SESSION**
	Moderator:
	Jan van Schoonhoven, Senior Advisor to the UNECE on Public-Private Partnership
	Welcome speech:
	Bakytzhan Sagintayev, Minister of Economic Development and Trade of the Republic of Kazakhstan
	Zhomart Abiyessov, Chairman of the Board «Kazakhstan Public-Private Partnership Center» JSC
	Speakers:
	Eric Maskin, Nobel Prize winner in Economics 2007, "for having laid the foundations of mechanism design theory", Professor of Princeton University, USA

	Sir John Stuttard, Deputy Chairman of Advisory Board PricewaterhouseCoopers LLP
	Lee Youn Ho, Ambassador of International Economy and Trade
15:15-16:00	**DISCUSSION SESSION**
	Speakers:
	Anand Chiplunkar, Director of Urban Development and Water Division in the Central and West Asia Department (ADB), the Philippines
	Alexandr Bazhenov, Director of Public-Private Partnership Center, Vnesheconombank, Russian Federation
	Geoffrey Hamilton, Chief of Cooperation and Partnerships Section UNECE
	Kazuo Ueda, President of Japan PFI/PPP Association
16:30-17:50	**DISCUSSION SESSION (CONTINUATION)**
	Moderator:
	Zhomart Abiyessov, Chairman of the Board «Kazakhstan Public-Private Partnership Center» JSC
	Speakers:
	Zouheir Chebl, Senior Vice-President of "SNC-Lavalin International Inc", Canada
	Nurlan Dossayev, Financial Director of "ATM Group"
	Jill Jamieson, Head of USAID Macroeconomic Project
	James Cercone, Manager of the Healthcare technology transfer project of World Bank in the Republic of Kazakhstan, President of "Sanigest Internacional"
	Igor Abramov, Council at Heenan Blaikie, Canada
	Timur Pulatov, Head of Transaction Advisory Services at "Ernst & Young"
17:50-18:00	**Signing of Memoranda**

15:00-18:00 Palace of Independence, Conference Hall 1 (Picture Gallery), 1st Floor	**ROUND TABLE PERSPECTIVES FOR DEVELOPMENT OF TRANSPORT INFRASTRUCTURE IN KAZAKHSTAN**
	Organizer: Ministry of Transport and Communications of the Republic of Kazakhstan
	Questions for discussion: *- Ensuring needs of economy and population in qualitative transport services.* *- Developing and improving transport operation indicators in road and railway sectors.* *- Developing new forms of implementing concession projects, including PPP mechanisms.* *- Mobilizing investments into transport infrastructure.* *- Developing transit and logistic potential of the Republic of Kazakhstan.* *- Further developing of infrastructure in the civil aviation and sea vehicle sectors of the Republic of Kazakhstan.*

	 Azat Bekturov, Vice Minister of Transport and Communications of the Republic of Kazakhstan
	Mohammad Yahya Maroofi, Economic Cooperation Organization Secretary General
	Igor Rounov, Head of IRU Permanent Delegation to Eurasia
	Askar Mamin, President of "Kazakhstan Temir Zholy" National Company JSC
	Zamir Saginov, Chairman of Road Committee under the Ministry of Transport and Communications of the Republic of Kazakhstan
	Dastan Soltanbayev, Vice-President, "Kaztemirtrans" JSC
	Sergey Kulnazarov, Director General of "KazAeroNavigation" State-Run Enterprise
	Murat Bekmagambetov, President of "Research Institute for Transport and Communications" Ltd
	Teodor Kaplan, Secretary General, Union of International Road Carriers of the Republic of Kazakhstan
	Edil Iskakov, President, "Kedentransservice" JSC
	Berik Uandykov, Director of "Aktau International Trade Seaport" State-Run Enterprise
	Marat Saduov, TRACECA IGC PS National Secretary for Kazakhstan
	Raimondo Betti, Head of Construction and Engineering Mechanics Department, Columbia University, USA
	Erkhat Iskaliev, Vice-President of JSC "NC "Kazakhstan Temir Zholy" Logistics

16:00-17:00 Palace of Independence Conference Hall 2 (Picture Gallery), 1st Floor	**PANEL SESSION** **RAPID GROWTH MARKETS FORECAST, INVESTMENT ATTRACTIVENESS OF KAZAKHSTAN**
	Questions for discussion: *- Rising importance of rapid-growth markets.* *- Kazakhstan attractiveness profile: perception of 200 prospective and existing investors from 27 countries.* *- Restoring the banking sector: how non-performing loans are addressed across Europe and Kazakhstan.*
	 Kairat Kelimbetov, Deputy Prime Minister of the Republic of Kazakhstan
	Karl Johansson, CIS Managing Partner, Ernst & Young
	Lars Nyberg, President and CEO, TeliaSonera
	Lorenzo Simonelli, President and CEO, GE Transportation

	Olivier Descamps, Business Group Director, Southern and Eastern Europe, Caucasus and Central Asia, EBRD
	Marcia Favale, Senior Advisor to the Prime Minister of the Republic of Kazakhstan
	Alexander Yerofeev, Partner, CIS Head of Restructuring, Ernst & Young

17:30-18:45 Palace of Independence, Conference Hall 2 (Picture Gallery), 1st Floor	**DIALOGUE WITH NOURIEL ROUBINI PROSPECTS FOR THE GLOBAL ECONOMY**
	Organizer: "Eurasian Economic Club of Scientists" Association
	Moderator: **Kairat Kelimbetov,** Deputy Prime Minister of the Republic of Kazakhstan
	Speaker: **Nouriel Roubini,** President of RGE Monitor Company, American Economist, Professor of New York University, Chairman of Roubini Global Economics, USA

Where can you find interesting stories about investments, export and trade on the internet?

Nurbek Achilov has some resources for you!

On Blogger's platform he runs his blog about investments, export, trade and other issues.

Blog about investment, export and trade in English:

https://nurbekachilov.blogspot.com/

Blog about investment, export and trade in English:

https://nurbekachil.blogspot.com/

You can also find ideas, photos and experiences about investments, trade and investment on Nurbek Achilov's pages in Facebook, Instagram, Pinterest, Slideshare,

Academia and LinkedIn and other accounts.

orcid.org/0000-0003-1238-6556

Tips for Travelers

Nurbek Achilov

Second Edition

Get this new book with the Special Price on Amazon.com

200 web-sites and tools for online presence

Essential Handbook for marketing and growth

Nurbek Achilov

First Edition

Handbook for Marketing Students

Best tips and strategies

Nigel Aksel

First Edition